Great Explorations in Math and Science (GEMS) Program

The Lawrence Hall of Science (LHS) is a public science center on the University of California at Berkeley campus. LHS offers a full program of activities for the public, including workshops and classes, exhibits, films, lectures, and special events. LHS is also a center for teacher education and curriculum research and development.

Over the years, LHS staff have developed a multitude of activities, assembly programs, classes, and interactive exhibits. These programs have proven to be successful at the Hall and should be useful to schools, other science centers, museums, and community groups. A number of these guided-discovery activities have been published under the Great Explorations in Math and Science (GEMS) title, after an extensive refinement and adaptation process that includes classroom testing of trial versions, modifications to ensure the use of easy-to-obtain materials, with carefully written and edited step-by-step instructions and background information to allow presentation by teachers without special background in mathematics or science.

Staff
Glenn T. Seaborg, **Principal Investigator**
Jacqueline Barber, **Director**
Kimi Hosoume, **Associate Director**
Cary Sneider, **Science Curriculum Specialist**
Jaine Kopp, **Mathematics Curriculum Specialist**
Carolyn Willard, **GEMS Sites and Centers Coordinator**
Laura Tucker, **GEMS Workshop Coordinator**
Lynn Barakos, Katharine Barrett, Kevin Beals, Ellen Blinderman,
Beatrice Boffen, Celia Cuomo, Gigi Dornfest, John Erickson,
Stan Fukunaga, Philip Gonsalves, Cathy Larripa, Linda Lipner,
Laura Lowell, Stephen Rutherford, Debra Sutter, Rebecca Tilley,
Staff Development Specialists
Cynthia Eaton, **Administrative Coordinator**
Karen Milligan, **Distribution Coordinator**
Terry Cort, **Workshop Administrator**
Felicia Roston, **Distribution Representative**
Bryan Burd, George Kasarjian, **Shipping Assistants**
Stephanie Van Meter, **Trial Testing Coordinator**
Lisa Haderlie Baker, **Art Director**
Carol Bevilacqua, Rose Craig, Lisa Klofkorn, **Designers**
Gerri Ginsburg, **Public Information Representative**
Lincoln Bergman, **Principal Editor**
Carl Babcock, **Senior Editor**
Florence Stone, **Assistant Editor**
Kay Fairwell, **Principal Publications Coordinator**
Larry Gates, Nancy Lin, Karla Penuelas, Alisa Sramala,
Staff Assistants

Contributing Authors
Jacqueline Barber
Katharine Barrett
Kevin Beals
Lincoln Bergman
Beverly Braxton
Kevin Cuff
Celia Cuomo
Linda De Lucchi
Gigi Dornfest
Jean Echols
Philip Gonsalves
Jan M. Goodman
Alan Gould
Kimi Hosoume
Susan Jagoda
Jaine Kopp
Linda Lipner
Laura Lowell
Larry Malone
Cary I. Sneider
Craig Strang
Debra Sutter
Rebecca Tilley
Jennifer Meux White
Carolyn Willard

Reviewers

We would like to thank the following educators who reviewed, tested, or coordinated the reviewing of *this series* of GEMS materials in manuscript and draft form (including the GEMS guides *Secret Formulas* and *Learning About Learning*). Their critical comments and recommendations, based on classroom presentation of these activities nationwide, contributed significantly to these GEMS publications. Their participation in the review process does not necessarily imply endorsement of the GEMS program or responsibility for statements or views expressed. This role is an invaluable one; feedback is carefully recorded and integrated as appropriate into the publications. **THANK YOU!**

Alaska

Iditarod Elementary School, Wasilla
Tacy Carr
Cynthia Dolmas Curran*
Carol Lowery
Bonnie Tesar

Arizona

Hualapai Elementary School, Kingman
Nora Brown
Catherine Ann Claes*
Traci A. D'Arcy
Rhonda Gilbert
Lisa Julle*
Barbara McLarty
Stephanie L. Murillo
Rose Roberts

Northern Arizona University, Flagstaff
Lynda Hatch**

California

Albany Middle School, Albany
Jenny Anderson
Chiyo Masuda
Kay Sorg*
Janet Teel

Beacon Day School, Oakland
Deborah Ellis

Claremont Middle School, Oakland
Susan Cristancho*
Malia Dinell-Schwartz
Sheila Lucia
Mike Predovic

Dover Middle School, Fairfield
Rebecca Hammond
Sarah Yourd

Fairmont Elementary School, El Cerrito
Nancy Buckingham
Carrie Cook*
Karen DeTore
Sandi Healy
Linda Lambie*
Katy Miles
Laura Peck
Nancy Rutter-Spriggs

Foshay Learning Center, Los Angeles
Stephanie Hoffman*

Golden State Middle School, West Sacramento
Natasha Lowrie

Jefferson Elementary School, Berkeley
Mary Ann Furuichi
Linda Mengel*
Fern Stroud
Gaye Ying

Malcolm X Intermediate School, Berkeley
Arden Clute
DeEtte LaRue
Mahalia Ryba*

Marina Middle School, Los Angeles
Leticia Escajeda

Markham Elementary School, Oakland
Eleanor Feuille
Sharon Kerr*
Ruth Quezada
Audry Taylor
Margaret Wright

Nelson Elementary School, Pinedale
Julia Hollenbeck
Vicki Jackson
Erla Stanley
Phyllis Todd*

Nobel Middle School, Northridge
Margie Hickman

Oxford School, Berkeley
Anita Baker*
Mary Barrett
Joe Brulenski
Barbara Edwards
Judy Kono

Park Day School, Oakland
Aggie Brenneman
Karen Corzan*
Michelle McAfee Krueger
Suzie McLean-Balderston

Parker Elementary School, Oakland
Lorynne Dupree
Linda Rogers*
Zepita Sharp
Marian Wilson

Washington Irving Middle School, Los Angeles
Mary Lu Camacho
Bernadette J. Cullen
Joe Kevany
Thomas Yee*

Westside Science Center, Los Angeles
Nonnie Korten**

Willard Junior High School, Berkeley
Kathy Evan
Clydine James

Colorado

Franklin Elementary School, Sterling
Vickie Baseggio
Marty Belknap
Barbara Nelson
Shelly Stumpf*

District of Columbia

Anne Beers Elementary School, Washington, D.C.
Elizabeth Dortch
Fredric Hutchinson
Gloria McKenzie-Freeman
Connie Parker*
Gregory Taylor
Gloria Warren Tucker**

Maine

Coastal Ridge Elementary School, York
Nancy Annis
Rick Comeau**
Julie Crafts
Patricia Gray
Carol A. Moody

York Middle School, York
Andrew Berenson
Deborah J. Bradburn
Rick Comeau**
Jean Dominguez
Susan E. Miller
Robert G. Vincent

Michigan

Marine City Middle School, Marine City
Peggy Brooks*
Gina Day
Laura Newton
Alan Starkey

North Carolina

C. W. Stanford Middle School, Hillsborough
Leslie Kay Jones*
Tom Kuntzleman
Christopher Longwill
Dawn M. Wills

Grady Brown Elementary School, Hillsborough
Lisa A. Crocker
Audrey T. Johnson
Sandra Kosik
Sandra L. McKee*
Tonya L. Price
Karen Sexton

* On-Site Coordinator
** Regional Coordinator

Contents

Acknowledgments

These activities derive from a wealth of imaginative and inventive activities presented by the Chemistry Education Department of the Lawrence Hall of Science over the past decade. These classes have included young children devising their "secret formulas" for many products, including those featured in this guide. The two main authors would like to thank many current Chemistry Department staff members who have been most helpful in commenting on or doing research for this publication, including Laura Lowell, the Director of Chemistry Education, Lynn Barakos, Kevin Beals, Anne Brocchini, and Jennifer Seiler. Anne and Jennifer were particularly helpful in reviewing the entire guide and contributing substantially to the revision of the rock salt and ice cream activities. Two former Chemistry staff members, Mayumi Shinohara and Lisa Walenceus, helped inspire early versions of these activities. Angelica Stacy, Professor of Chemistry at the University of California at Berkeley, was kind enough to review this guide for accuracy and chemistry content.

Jacqueline Barber, the GEMS Director, provided key critique and overview of the main educational elements of the activities. Both she and GEMS Principal Editor Lincoln Bergman contributed to the text in diverse ways. Florence Stone, the GEMS Assistant Editor, played an active part in the classroom testing observation process, and ensured the editorial consistency of this detailed unit. Alisa Sramala did an outstanding job of gathering and organizing the massive (and ever-changing) trial test kits for these activities. Special thanks to Cynthia Eaton and Stephanie Van Meter for coordination of the trial testing process, and to Cynthia as well for research on the availability of calcium carbonate for the toothpaste activities.

A number of individuals and companies assisted us with the testing and related research of this materials-rich unit. Nancy Lovre of SmithKlein Beecham, the makers of TUMS, arranged for the generous donation of 7,200 TUMS tablets used in testing. George Ball, President of W. Atlee Burpee & Company, generously donated seed packets that were used in testing of a potting soil activity that was not included in the final guide. Jeff Melendy of Birite Foodservice Distributors assisted us in ordering large quantities of materials more economically. Ken Thompson, a chemist at Sargent-Welch, was particularly helpful in clarifying the issues regarding food grade calcium carbonate. David Hakes,

President of Chem Lab Supplies, agreed to offer food grade calcium carbonate at a discount when used by teachers for these activities. We also spoke to Garry Rittershaus of Tom's of Maine regarding calcium carbonate.

We would also like to note that we first saw the use of ziplock bags for mixing ice cream in an activity published by Project Storyline: Science, entitled "The 'Scoop' on Matter," distributed through the California Science Implementation Network (CSIN). That activity focuses on the changes that take place as ice cream is made, and serves as a culminating assessment activity for a unit on matter.

Judy Chandler, a teacher at Ohlone School in Hercules, California, was kind enough to lend us her class for the first author-taught classroom versions of these activities. The authors would finally like to thank and dedicate their efforts to all the eager students and willing teachers who assisted us in refining the activities in this guide. These teachers are listed in the front of the guide. Their comments and the student work they often included with their feedback were invaluable.

The process that students engage in during these activities parallels some aspects of what scientists and inventors do as they develop new products and innovations. As part of the process of bringing a product to market and protecting it from unauthorized imitation, companies legally register their product names. Because so many products are mentioned or used in *Secret Formulas*, we've chosen to note these legal registrations in the front of this guide. When these products are referred to in the text, the following registered trademarks are understood:

Coca-Cola® and Coca-Cola Classic® are registered trademarks of The Coca-Cola Company

Colgate® is a registered trademark of Colgate-Palmolive Company

Elmer's® Glue-All is a registered trademark of Borden, Inc.

Glad® is a registered trademark of First Brands Corporation

Ivory Snow® Detergent is a registered trademark of Procter & Gamble

M&M's® Brand Chocolate Candies is a registered trademark of M&M/Mars, a division of Mars, Inc.

Pepsi® is a registered trademark of Pepsico, Inc.

Post-it® Brand Notes is a registered trademark of 3M

Solo® is a registered trademark of Solo Cup Company

Tom's of Maine® is a registered trademark of Tom's of Maine, Inc.

TUMS® is a registered trademark of SmithKline Beecham Consumer Healthcare

Velcro® is a registered trademark of Velcro USA, Inc.

ZIPLOC® is a registered trademark of DowBrands

Introduction

In *Secret Formulas*, young students become laboratory scientists *and* creative inventors as they make their own paste, toothpaste, cola, and ice cream. In the case of each "product," they follow the same sequence of science processes—they study the attributes of the product, test its ingredients, and then mix ingredients to create their own personal "secret formula."

Children love to mix things together to make something else. Whether it's mud, grass, or a sprinkling of flower pollen, the special ingredients they put in a mixture make it a unique, personal creation. And who knows what it might become—maybe something entirely different! The idea that *anything* could happen is one reason mixing ingredients to make "potions" is so fascinating in childhood and a part of so many fables and stories.

The *Secret Formulas* unit allows students the opportunity to focus on observing and describing the properties and attributes of substances. It also gives students the repeated opportunities they need to understand and begin to use the concept of cause and effect in their investigations. With experience and experimentation, the students learn that certain outcomes are dependable, repeatable, and have logical causes. This deepening comprehension of cause and effect is in turn essential to their development and understanding of controlled experimentation in later grades.

Attributes and Properties

In describing substances, students of this age will naturally list a substance's properties as well as other attributes. A *property* can be seen, heard, smelled, or felt by the senses. Properties of toothpaste may include, for example, its minty taste, its pasty and slightly gritty consistency, or its white color. *Attributes* are descriptors, detailing the properties, qualities, character, and characteristics of a substance. Attributes of toothpaste include the above list of properties *and* other attributes, such as: that it is used to brush teeth; is sometimes stored in a tube; often has fluoride in it; is recommended by dentists; and shouldn't be swallowed. Attributes go beyond the physical and chemical properties of a substance. The broad focus on attributes is appropriate to this age. Students will get lots of practice in observing, comparing, and communicating as they investigate the attributes of both the ingredients they use and the products they make. They'll also have fun making attribute riddles!

Repeatability of Results

In order to understand the concept of *cause and effect,* it is necessary to first understand the idea that if we follow a formula exactly, adding the same ingredients in the same amounts, the outcome will always be the same. This concept of *repeatability of results* is so fundamental to science, and is so much taken for granted in our own mental frameworks that we don't always realize that **it needs to be learned.** A teacher once asked her five-year-old students, "If I blow a bubble, will it go up or down?" They gave their predictions with thumbs—half the thumbs pointed up and half pointed down. She blew the bubble and they watched it float downwards. She again asked for their predictions: would the bubble go up or down? Many students still predicted that the bubble would go up. She continued allowing them to predict and having them watch what happened. Not until she blew the *fifth* bubble, and they all watched it float downwards for the *fifth* time, were *all* students convinced that the next bubble would "for sure" go down. It wasn't obvious to them that it would always happen that way! It takes repeated evidence to build this notion. While some of your students will come to this unit having a sense of this concept, all of your students will deepen their understanding that results are repeatable.

Cause and Effect

Once students know that results are dependable, they can begin to focus on the specific cause of a certain result or effect, and the relationship between them. "When I add more rock salt, the ice water gets colder!" "The more glycerin I add, the oozier my toothpaste gets!" "If your cola is too sweet, try adding more lime juice. It makes it taste more sour!" This process of ferreting out what causes certain effects will help students build the foundation they'll need for later years, when they begin to conduct controlled experiments by systematically changing one ingredient (or variable) at a time. For now, being systematic is less important than having students investigate the attributes of ingredients and how these cause their final product to have certain, predictable attributes.

Session-by-Session Overview

Secret Formulas has nine sessions, one for paste, three for cola, three for toothpaste, and two for ice cream. In Session 1, students learn the word *ingredient* and explore four possible ingredients for paste. They do a "sticky test" to determine which ingredient sticks the best, then mix together several ingredients to make a personal paste, and use it to make a class bar graph. One goal of this first session is to give students the opportunity to learn and practice skills they will use throughout the unit: how to measure both dry and wet ingredients, and how to share materials and work in a group of four. The students do not record their formulas for paste; later in the unit, they will discover the need for careful record-keeping in science, and they will create a written formula for each of the later products.

In Sessions 2, 3, and 4, students become cola scientists. In the first of these sessions, they get a taste of a commercial cola, make a list of its attributes, and write attribute "riddles." In Session 3, students taste three mystery sugar water mixtures and discover cause and effect directly—the more sugar, the sweeter a mixture tastes. Next, students are challenged to make a sugar water mixture that matches the sweetness of commercial cola. The students must now depend on the idea that if the sweetness matches, then the number of spoonfuls of sugar must be the same. Finally, in Session 4, the students make their own cola formulas, using what they learned about the optimal amount of sugar, and adding other ingredients, like vanilla, cinnamon, and lime juice. They record the ingredients and amounts they used on a student data sheet.

The sequence of observing, testing, and then creating a personal formula is repeated for toothpaste in Sessions 5, 6, and 7. Students get a little taste of commercial toothpaste in Session 5, list attributes of toothpaste, and write attribute "riddles." Also in Session 5, they test four ingredients of toothpaste to find out which foams the best and which has the best consistency. In Session 6, students test the same four ingredients to see which cleans the best. In Session 7, they mix ingredients in a sandwich bag to make their own personal toothpaste, recording their formula as they create it. They take home a bit of personal toothpaste to use that night.

By now they have become good measurers, understand that the ingredients they choose have a predictable effect, and are "old pros" at recording their creations as they make them: your students are ready to become ice cream scientists! In Session 8, they study the effect of rock salt on the temperature of ice. In a "hands-on" experience, groups of students feel temperature differences and see which mixture is best to freeze little bags of water. In the last, culminating session, they choose and mix ice cream ingredients in a small sandwich bag, put that into a larger bag of ice and rock salt, and then shake it to transform it into ice cream. Each group of four students actually shakes the ice cream inside a T-shirt "sling." When they open their bags, all they need is a spoon to enjoy the delicious fruits of their scientific labor. And after the last spoonful is gone, they still have their secret formula recorded on paper, just in case they'd like to make their personal ice cream another time.

Assessment Suggestions and Literature Connections

Secret Formulas, like all GEMS guides, includes special sections on assessment and literature connections. The "Assessment Suggestions" outline selected student learning outcomes, describe ways that assessment tasks are built into these activities, and list additional assessment ideas. The "Literature Connections" section highlights books that make strong connections to the learning in these activities. We welcome your suggestions.

"Summary Outlines," including detailed preparation checklists in the "Getting Ready" sections, are provided to assist you in preparing and presenting the activities. Additional, removable copies of student data sheets are also included. A "Behind the Scenes" background section, organized by product (paste, cola, toothpaste, ice cream), with some interesting information on inventions, is intended to assist you in considering questions students may have.

Lots of Mathematics Too!

The major mathematics strands that interweave throughout these activities are listed on the title page, and throughout the guide we have included marginal notes and "Going Further" ideas that suggest ways to bring out different mathematical emphases. As they eagerly get their "hands-on" all the activities in this guide, students are developing measurement skills and related concepts. This is a strong and natural emphasis in this guide, and many real-life connections abound. The experience students gain with measurement in this unit centers on non-standard units of measure, such as spoons, straw droppers, and toothpicks. This is a wonderful way to prepare students for using standard units of measure. Another aspect of measurement that is woven through the activities is comparison. To determine their own secret formulas, students compare ingredients and their attributes to come up with the ideal proportions for their "personal favorite" formula.

In the paste session the results of student tests are graphed, then discussed and evaluated. Additional graphing possibilities are suggested throughout the unit. Students gain valuable, basic experience in graphing data in context and evaluating their results through concrete, visual, mathematical display. "Going Further" suggestions for both cola and toothpaste include a preference graph of favorite colas/toothpastes—giving students early experience with the many ways graphs can be used in statistics. Numbers are also used in context throughout the unit, as students determine, for example, the number of spoonfuls of corn starch to make their ideal paste or the number of drops of vanilla needed for their own special cola. Another "Going Further" invites students to compare and evaluate reasons for the prices of different toothpastes, introducing mathematical analysis as a central focus in the growing field of consumer science and the always-crucial demands of tight family budgets!

There are many other math-related teaching opportunities in this guide, and we'd love to hear your ideas. Perhaps most importantly, the activities in this guide can provide a solid and compelling sense to students and teachers of the inextricable connection between math and science. As such it is an excellent example of what science and mathematics educators mean by "the integration of math and science." And all of this mathematical learning is multiplied logarithmically by the high level of student involvement!

Important Comment on Preparation

Given the nature of this unit, a great deal of preparation is involved. Immediately following this introduction, we've added a special section on creating a basic kit for these activities, with other suggestions for easing and organizing the many tasks involved. Please read that section carefully and adapt to your own conditions as necessary. Team teaching and other modes of coordinating presentation with a larger group of teachers in your school or district is, of course, highly advantageous. **Obtaining volunteer help from aides, parents, or older students will be of immense value!**

We have also made an intensive effort to organize preparation in stages, for example: weeks or days before the activity; the day before the activity; and the day of the activity. You may want to modify these even further, depending on your circumstances. Some portions of steps we may have placed the day before the activity, for example, could also be done further ahead of time. We recommend doing as much preparation as is possible well ahead of time, especially the first time you present the unit. We suggest some shortcuts and offer tips for saving time. We welcome your ideas, and will consider each and every suggestion you make when this guide is revised.

One school district involved in testing this unit became so enthusiastic that they requested special permission to include Secret Formulas *as an official component of their curriculum even before this guide was published. They found effective ways to handle the preparation, were overwhelmed at the positive teacher and student reaction, and felt this kind of activity-based unit truly made science come alive for their students.*

One thing is certain—teachers who have presented this unit overwhelmingly agreed that the preparation is well worth it—the wealth of student learning in science, mathematics, and real-world technology combined with intense student interest and enthusiasm makes *Secret Formulas* an extraordinarily memorable educational experience!

Conclusion

As the magical idea that *anything* could happen fades, a new comprehension of the power of science emerges. Now, as scientists, the students learn to predict the effects of certain ingredients, to understand their interactions, and to control the outcomes. They learn to appreciate that through observation, experimentation, and creative thinking, scientists really *can* make mixtures with exciting possibilities! And, it's still true, in a different way, that *anything* can happen—the horizons of science, the genius of human invention, and the creative wellsprings of our students are filled with limitless possibilities!

Time Frame

The times listed below are estimated. Times will vary depending on your circumstances and your particular group of students.

Making a "Basic Set" for *Secret Formulas*
Preparation   30 minutes

Session 1: What Makes Paste?
Preparation   60 minutes
Classroom Activity   60 minutes

Session 2: Tasting and Describing Cola
Preparation   15 minutes
Classroom Activity   45–60 minutes

Session 3: Investigating an Ingredient of Cola
Preparation   60 minutes
Classroom Activity   60 minutes

Session 4: Secret Formulas for Cola
Preparation   45 minutes
Classroom Activity   50 minutes

**Session 5: Tasting, Describing,
and Testing Toothpaste**
Preparation   15 minutes
Classroom Activity   35 minutes

Session 6: Testing More Toothpaste Ingredients
Preparation   50 minutes
Classroom Activity   65 minutes

Session 7: Secret Formulas for Toothpaste
Preparation   30 minutes
Classroom Activity   50 minutes

Session 8: Ice Cream Testing
Preparation   50 minutes
Classroom Activity   25 minutes

Session 9: Secret Formulas for Ice Cream
Preparation   35 minutes
Classroom Activity   55 minutes

Please be advised that preparing for Session 1 may take longer than 60 minutes the first time you do it, until you become more familiar with the methods. Once the basic way we've organized the unit is clear, preparation becomes more straightforward in subsequent sessions and much easier when you do the unit the next time! Send us your time-saving tips!

Creating Your Basic Secret Formulas *Kit*

Overview

This section guides you in assembling a class set of trays, cups, spoons, stirrers, and other items that your young scientists will use repeatedly throughout the nine sessions of this *Secret Formulas* unit.

Because students get to measure and mix **lots** of ingredients, *Secret Formulas* requires more than the average number of materials, with more preparation and clean-up. This special section on creating a basic kit is designed to assist you in presenting this unit as inexpensively and efficiently as possible. In addition to creating the basic kit, we have included many other suggestions, all designed to streamline preparation and reduce clean-up time.

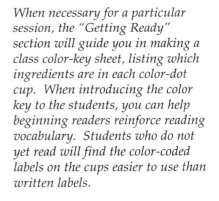

You'll put together a class set of color-coded plastic cups, spoons, stirrers, and "droppers" that your students will use over and over for different class sessions. It will of course be necessary to wash or rinse the cups after each session. Still, that extra effort is balanced by lower costs for cups and labels, and less waste.

Most of the materials for the *Secret Formulas* basic kit and for the additional items needed throughout the unit should be available at a supermarket or a large drug store. However, some may need to be special ordered, donated, or purchased at a different store. The "Sources for Materials" section on page 114 has information about these materials.

Teachers who have taught the *Secret Formulas* unit say that the results are well worth the extra effort of obtaining and managing materials. Their strongest pieces of advice are:

When necessary for a particular session, the "Getting Ready" section will guide you in making a class color-key sheet, listing which ingredients are in each color-dot cup. When introducing the color key to the students, you can help beginning readers reinforce reading vocabulary. Students who do not yet read will find the color-coded labels on the cups easier to use than written labels.

- **Get some of the materials donated if possible.** Many of the materials are kitchen ingredients that many households have on hand. You may want to use a letter like the "Sample Letter to Parents" on page 116 to ask for materials.

- **Plan ahead.** Read the "Getting Ready" section for each session well in advance, and allow time to do some of the preparation before the day of the activity.

• **Share the preparation and materials.** Invite a colleague to teach the unit concurrently so you can share preparation and materials. **If at all possible, get an adult volunteer or two to help with set up, classroom activities, and clean up throughout the unit.** Many teachers use older students as helpers, too. In Session 9, when students make ice cream, an adult volunteer (or two or more!) is essential.

Whether you put together this basic kit yourself or have a volunteer do it for you, it will be an excellent investment of time. Every class session calls for some or all of these materials, so you'll always have a head start on your preparation. That way, you'll be better able to concentrate on gathering/organizing the remaining supplies and focus on presenting the activities.

What You Need (for a class of 32)

❐ 8 cafeteria trays*
❐ about 144 (12 dozen) three-ounce paper cups ("bathroom refill" type, but **not** the kind with pleated sides)
❐ 108 (9 dozen) clear, plastic cups (8 to 10 ounce size)
❐ about 120 (10 dozen) stick-on (self-adhesive) colored dots* about 20 each of: red, blue, yellow, green, and orange. Any diameter of dot is fine.
❐ 48 small, lightweight plastic spoons* (about $1/2$ teaspoon size)
❐ 60 plastic drinking straws (unwrapped, not the kind that bend) *or* 120 disposable medicine droppers* *or* 32 washable medicine droppers*
❐ about 36 plastic stirrers
❐ about 72 popsicle sticks
❐ 8 containers (cottage cheese-type, about 1 pint)
❐ 168 (14 dozen) ziplock sandwich bags

*For these items, please see the "Sources for Materials" section, page 114.

Important Notes

Cafeteria trays: Trays make it much easier to organize the materials, and are essential for quick distribution and collection of the many cups of ingredients your students will be using. Sturdy, plastic ones the size of those used in fast-food restaurants or larger are ideal.

Clear plastic cups: We recommend Solo brand, wide-mouthed, 9-ounce "squat" cups. Because they are made from flexible plastic, they can be washed and re-used many times without cracking. They are available in most supermarkets.

Plastic Spoons: There are two sizes of plastic spoons commonly available. The lightweight ones are smaller, and equivalent to about $1/2$ teaspoon. The larger, heavyweight spoons are equivalent to a scant one teaspoon. We recommend the smaller, lightweight spoons so students will need to use more spoonfuls, and will get more practice measuring! These smaller spoons are usually available at wholesale paper goods stores, large discount stores, etc. If you can't find the lightweight spoons, the heavier ones will do, but you'll need to halve the amounts of powders (the number of spoonfuls) the students measure.

Getting Ready

Label the "personal" tasting cups.

1. Your students will frequently need to taste ingredients or mixtures, so they'll need a personal cup. Use a permanent marker to write each student's initials (or name) on a clear plastic cup. **The location of the initials is important because, at times, students will need to fill their cups with three ounces of liquid.** To make that easier, write their initials so the **bottoms of the letters are on the three-ounce point** of the cup.

2. To find the three-ounce point, fill a three-ounce paper cup with water (or use a measuring cup), pour it into a plastic cup, and make a mark at the water line. Once you have one plastic cup marked, you can use a ruler to mark the rest, or just estimate with a visual comparison to the first cup.

Color code the ingredient cups.

1. You won't need to use this whole set of color-coded plastic cups right away, but it's easiest to make them all now. To color code the cups, apply a self-adhesive colored dot to the side of each. Of course, any different colored dots would do, but since the colors below are referred to throughout the nine sessions, try to choose dots that match them if possible. This way, following the guide's instructions will be as easy as possible.

2. Save the extra dots for use in making charts and labeling bags later. For now, just store the whole class set of labeled cups stacked by color. Later, take the ones you need for each session, and sort them on cafeteria trays for the student groups. **Make enough total cups so that each group of four students can have:**

- two red-dot cups (two cups, each with one red dot)
- one blue-dot cup
- one yellow-dot cup
- one green-dot cup
- one orange-dot cup
- one **half**-dot yellow cup
- one **half**-dot green cup

Some teachers prefer to cut the straws to $^3/_4$ length, finding that makes them somewhat easier to use. This of course uses more straws. In our testing, we've had no problems with straws cut at half-length, but wanted to let you know about this option.

3. **Make straws into droppers.** (If you're using real medicine droppers, you can skip this step.) Cut all the straws in half. A good way to do this without having straws fly all over the room, is to put a rubber band around a handful at a time, and use scissors or a paper cutter to cut the whole bundle at once.

4. You will need to obtain **calcium carbonate powder for the toothpaste activities.** Either prepare to grind up TUMS or to order calcium carbonate. See the "Sources for Materials" section on page 114, or the note near the "Getting Ready" headings in Sessions 5 and 7 for more information on grinding up TUMS or the ordering option.

Congratulations!
You have just created
Your *Secret Formulas* Basic Kit!

A basic kit

Can be key

To presenting this unit

Successfully.

Session 1: What Makes Paste?

Overview

In this session, students learn that *ingredients* are things that we can mix together to make something—in this case, paste! Students begin by observing and testing four possible ingredients for paste: baking soda, flour, cornstarch, and salt. Students measure the powders, mix each of them with water, do a test for stickiness, and share results with their teammates. At the end of the session, each student gets a chance to choose one or more of the ingredients then mix them with water to make their own "personal pastes." They use their pastes to build a class bar graph that reflects some of their findings.

The goal in the first session is for students to enjoy and experience the fundamental processes needed to develop any formula—first observing, measuring, and testing ingredients, and then mixing them together to make their own formulas and evaluating the results! For now, students are not asked to keep a tally of the amounts of ingredients they use or write down a formula. Later in the unit, students will discover for themselves the need for careful record-keeping in science.

The paste activities also give students the opportunity to learn and practice skills they will use throughout the unit: how to measure level spoonfuls of dry ingredients and how to use a "medicine dropper" made from half a drinking straw. They also become accustomed to working in groups of four, and sharing materials.

One teacher told us: "Students liked the paste session. At first I was unsure about whether the content of this session was worth the mess. Later, I saw that learning skills, such as measuring and using the droppers, was important… future sessions would have been much more difficult had these skills not been practiced."

Using non-standard measurement tools in this activity and throughout this unit gives students valuable experience and develops skills they can apply when they encounter standard measurement tools in math and science.

What You Need

For the class:

- ❒ 3 pieces of large white construction paper for class color key and graph (butcher paper or newsprint would also work)
- ❒ 4 wide-tipped felt markers in blue, yellow, green, and orange (four of the same colors as the stick-on dots)
- ❒ two colored dots each: red, blue, yellow, green, orange
- ❒ 2 boxes (about 16 oz.) of each: baking soda, table salt, cornstarch
- ❒ 2 lbs. white flour
- ❒ 1 stack of newspapers to cover table surfaces
- ❒ 2 sponges
- ❒ scissors or a paper cutter

For each group of four students:

- ❒ 1 cafeteria tray
- ❒ 1 set of 6 color-dot cups: red (2), blue, yellow, green, orange
- ❒ 4 small, lightweight plastic spoons
- ❒ 4 half-straws for droppers
- ❒ 8 popsicle sticks (4 to level, 4 to mix pastes)
- ❒ 8 small, sturdy paper cups, 3 oz. "bathroom refill" type (not the type with pleated sides); have a few extras on hand in case some tear during paste mixing
- ❒ 4 small pieces of white scratch paper or 3" x 5" cards
- ❒ 4 dried beans, uncooked, small, uniform size (black beans are fine)
- ❒ 4 1"-square scraps of construction paper
- ❒ 4 pencils
- ❒ 4 ziplock bags for students to take paste home
- ❒ a few damp paper towels for wiping sticky fingers

Some teachers decide to obtain real medicine droppers instead of the drinking straw droppers for this session and the rest of the unit. You'll find sources for real medicine droppers in the "Sources for Materials" section on page 114.

Getting Ready

Before the Day of the Activity

1. **Get volunteer help and donations of materials.** If possible, arrange for an adult or an older student to help during the activity, as well as during set up and clean up. You may want to use a letter like the "Sample Letter to Parents" on page 116 asking for donations of materials and volunteer time.

2. **Decide if you'll pre-teach the water-dropper technique.** One of the goals of this first class session is to give your students practice in using a dropper, which they will need throughout the unit. Older students may learn the technique fairly easily during the paste activity. Some teachers of younger students prefer to introduce the water droppers in a separate, earlier practice session. Practice using a dropper yourself. If you decide your young scientists need it, allow time for a practice session with just droppers and water.

3. **Think about room arrangement.** Students will need to be seated in groups of four for almost all sessions of *Secret Formulas.* You'll also need a large table or counter, preferably near a sink, to set up trays of materials.

Please look over the steps listed under "On the Day of the Activity" to see if there are more tasks you may be able to accomplish several days before the activity. Doing so will reduce time needed on the day of the activity itself. For example, the color coding of cups and class bar graph could be prepared ahead of time.

On the Day of the Activity

Materials on Trays

1. **Fill cups of ingredients.** On a cafeteria tray for each group, set out the six color-coded plastic cups listed below. Fill each cup about **half full** of the appropriate ingredient.
- **two** red-dot cups: water
- one blue-dot cup: baking soda
- one yellow-dot cup: salt
- one green-dot cup: flour
- one orange-dot cup: cornstarch

2. **Add measuring implements to the plastic cups.** Put a plastic spoon and a popsicle stick into each of the four cups of powders. Put two half-straws (or real medicine droppers) into each of the water cups.

Even if students will not use up a half cup of the powders, it is important to fill the cups half full so that students can scoop out the powders with their spoons more easily.

A way to cut straws in half without having them fly all over the room is to put a rubber band around a handful of straws before cutting them with either scissors or a paper cutter.

*For younger students, you may want to tape the straw droppers lightly into the bent position. (Please see the drawing and instructions on page 21.) Taping the droppers prevents anyone from accidentally using them as drinking straws **and makes them easier for small fingers to use!***

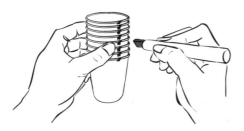

There are four extra paper cups per group, but they don't need to be color coded or put on the trays; just set them aside for now.

3. Color code the paper cups and add them to the trays. Color code four paper cups to match the four colors on the plastic cups: blue, yellow, green, and orange. A quick way to color code them is to take a permanent colored marker and swipe the tip along a stack of cups. As you draw the marker down over the stack, you'll leave a small dot of color on the lip of each cup. Put a set of four different-colored paper cups on each tray.

4. Add a few damp paper towels to each tray.

5. Set out the trays and demonstration materials. Have one tray of materials near where you will introduce the activity. Keep the other trays in a central location, ready to distribute when your introduction is over. If students will be gathered away from their seats at a rug area for your introduction, you could have the trays ready to use on their tables.

Materials Not on Trays

1. **Make a color code key for the class.** On a piece of white construction paper (or butcher paper or newsprint) list: water, baking soda, salt, flour, and cornstarch. Stick one of the appropriately colored dots on the key next to each ingredient (or color in larger circles of the same colors). Have the color key handy near where you will introduce the activity.

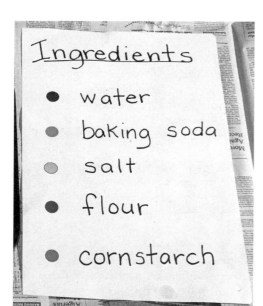

Ingredients
- water
- baking soda
- salt
- flour
- cornstarch

2. **Prepare the class bar graph.** Put four color dots (blue, green, yellow, and orange) along the short end of a piece of large white construction paper. Leave as much space as possible between dots. At the end of the session, the class will create a bar graph by using their paste to stick colored construction-paper squares above these colored dots. Have an extra piece of white construction paper handy in case the bar graph needs to be taller.

3. **Cut paper squares for the bar graph.** Cut enough 1" squares of construction paper so each student will have one to put on a class bar graph at the end of the session. Use any color(s) that will show up well against white.

4. **Prepare paper for the sticky test.** Cut a piece of 8 $1/2$" x 11" scratch paper into four quarters for each group of students (3" x 5" cards are also fine).

5. **Set aside remaining materials for later in the session.** Have handy, but not on the trays, the scratch paper, construction paper squares, pencils, beans, extra paper cups, sponges, newspaper, and ziplock bags.

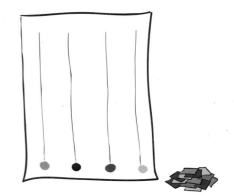

Introducing the Activity

1. Ask the students to raise their hands if they ever mixed lots of things together to make a secret potion or a secret formula. Tell them that the things people mix together to make something are called *"ingredients."* Ask, "What are some ingredients you might mix together to make soup?" [onions, potatoes, etc.] "What are some ingredients you might want to put in cookies?" [chocolate chips, sugar, nuts]

2. Discuss how scientists get to mix ingredients together to make many different things. Today the students will be scientists and mix some ingredients together to make paste. Ask, "What is paste used for?" [to stick or fasten things together]

3. Explain that they will be working in teams of four scientists, sharing a tray of materials, using different ingredients to see if they make paste. Say that their groups will mix four different powders with water to see which makes the best paste.

The well-known book Stone Soup *makes a nice connection to the idea of ingredients, as does* Vegetable Soup. *Both books are listed in the "Literature Connections" section, page 123.*

Explaining and Demonstrating the Procedure

1. Explain how to tell the different powders apart by finding the colored dots on the cups, and then looking at the color-coded key. Read the list of ingredients from the color-coded key, holding up the appropriate cup as you introduce each of the powders: baking soda, flour, salt, and cornstarch. Mention that students will also have two cups of water on their tray.

2. Tell the students that when they get their tray, the first thing their group will do is look carefully at their four powders. Emphasize that these ingredients are **not for eating or tasting,** because they may not have been kept clean.

3. Tell them that **each student in their group will get to test one of the powders** by mixing it with water in a paper cup. Emphasize that they will all get a chance later to mix more than one powder together, but not now.

Demonstrate Measuring the Powder

1. Ask the students, "If you get to test the powder from the blue-dot cup, which ingredient will you be testing?" [baking soda] Show the color-coded blue paper cup from your demonstration tray. Explain that they will put some of the powder into the paper cup to mix it with water.

2. Demonstrate how to measure two level spoonfuls of powder, showing how to flatten the powder in the spoon by using the popsicle stick as a "bulldozer." On the chalkboard, write a big "2" with a drawing of a spoon next to it to remind students how much powder to put into their paper cups.

3. Tell the class that it is hard to clean up powders if they spill on chairs, floor, etc. Emphasize the importance of being neat, careful scientists.

Demonstrate the Water-Dropper Technique

1. Demonstrate how to use a straw as a homemade medicine dropper:

    a. First, bend over the top third of the straw, and pinch the double part of the straw (not the fold).

    b. **Keep squeezing** as you lower the straw into the water.

    c. Stop squeezing. Then lift the straw out of the cup.

    d. Pinch a little bit at a time to make drops come out into another cup.

2. Ask students to imagine they have droppers in their hands and have them practice the procedure with you several times. A good basic "rule of squeeze" for them to remember is: **squeeze, unsqueeze, squeeze.** Then the steps relating to the liquid can be added:

    squeeze
    lower into the liquid
    unsqueeze
    lift out of liquid
    squeeze (squirt in this session, drops in others)

3. Repeat the sequence, using "imaginary water," until most of the students seem to understand how to use a dropper.

4. Tell students they should put as much water into their cup as it takes to make the powder wet, but not too soupy. Later in the unit, the students will add ingredients drop by drop, but for now, squirts are best.

Demonstrate Adding Water and Mixing

1. Tell the students that the two water cups on their trays are for the whole group to share. Each person will get a water dropper.

2. Without actually squirting water into the demonstration cup, show students how to add a few squirts of water to the powder, stir with the popsicle stick, and observe.

If you feel your students need practice with using water droppers, consider doing a short, preliminary practice session with just droppers and water. For older students, the practice they get during the paste activities will probably be enough.

Teachers of younger students sometimes tape the droppers lightly into the bent position to prevent them from being mistaken for drinking straws.

3. Ask the class, "What does paste need to be like so you'd want to use it?" "How would it feel, look, smell?" [Accept all answers, and be sure someone mentions stickiness.]

4. Tell students it is okay to touch the wet mixture with their fingers, and that they can wipe their fingers on the damp paper towels. Each student will observe the mixture they make, then pass the four cups around to everyone in their group.

Conducting the Ingredient Tests

1. Have one person from each team get newspapers to spread on their tables, and another get the tray of materials. Have teams begin.

2. Circulate, helping students use the droppers. As needed, encourage students by reminding them that the droppers take a little practice, but it's worth it, because they'll use the droppers in many fun activities.

3. When some groups have finished mixing and observing, give a two-minute warning to all groups to finish up. Circulate, asking students to show their cups to everyone in their group and talk about all four mixtures. Encourage students to think of good words to describe their mixtures. [bumpy, soggy, pasty] You may want to have them squish each mixture between their thumb and forefinger—does it feel sticky?

4. Ask groups to stop, set the materials on the table and put their hands in their laps. Ask, "What did you notice?" [There may be some contradictory observations; accept all answers.] Ask, "Were any of the mixtures sticky?" "How did they feel?" "Did you notice any smell?" and similar questions.

It is often difficult for teachers to get the attention of the whole class while the students have materials on their tables. For this reason, you might want to collect all the materials except their paper cups of "pastes" before introducing the sticky test, and redistribute them after you have introduced the Making Your "Personal Paste" activity.

Explaining the Sticky Test

1. Briefly explain that they will now get to do a test to find out which mixtures are sticky. Tell them they'll get to see how well a bean sticks to a piece of paper (or 3" x 5" card) using each of the four mixtures they made.

2. Demonstrate how to put a small dab on a piece of scratch paper (using finger or popsicle stick) as it lays flat on the table, and then place a bean on the dab. Each student will use the mixture they made, and they should leave the paper on the table until you give the signal.

3. Explain that when the class is ready, they'll lift the cards all at the same time (demonstrate lifting a piece of paper vertically, holding the paper by a corner). Ask for some predictions about what will happen when they lift up the papers. Will the bean stick?

4. When you are confident that students understand the sticky test, have a student from each group come and get four beans and four pieces of scratch paper.

Conducting the Sticky Test

1. Have students begin, using the mixture they made. When the entire class is ready, have them lift their papers.

2. If all or nearly all of the beans in their group stick, have students wave or gently shake their papers in the vertical position to see which sticks best.

3. Again, ask the class to set down their materials. Summarize class results by asking students to raise their hands if their group's "blue cup" mixture [baking soda] made the bean stick, if the "red cup" mixture did, etc. Which mixtures were the stickiest? Ask for any other observations about the flour, baking soda, corn starch, and salt. [spreadability, gooeyness, thickness] Mention that they'll get to vote on the ingredient they think is stickiest later.

4. Have a student go around and collect all the paper cups they've used already so they won't be tempted to mix the used materials with the new paste they're about to make.

Making Your "Personal Paste"

1. Ask, "Are you ready to make your own paste?" Say that each student will get a new paper cup for mixing. (No color coding needed this time.) They may want to mix more than one ingredient to make their own special paste, keeping in mind all they've learned about the ingredients.

2. Explain that they're limited to **five total spoonfuls** of powders. Can they use three spoonfuls of one and three of another? [No, that would add up to six!] They should think about it before starting. They can use as many squirts of water as they need, but you may want to remind them not to make it too soupy.

3. Have them begin. When all four students in a group have finished, collect all materials except their personal pastes.

This activity provides a great opportunity for young children to informally practice the "addition facts" for the number 5. Doing so in the context of this activity helps them see how these math facts are used and have meaning in a real-world context.

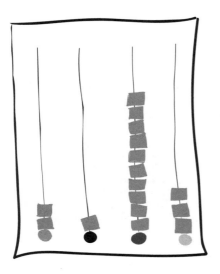

Graphing the Stickiest Ingredients and Cleaning Up

1. Before cleaning up, regain the attention of the class.

2. Tell students that during clean-up time, they will get to vote on which ingredient they thought was the stickiest. Show the graph you prepared earlier with the colored dots along the bottom edge.

3. Hold up a square of the construction paper you cut up earlier. Explain that each student will write their initials on one side of a paper square and put some of their personal paste on the other side. Explain that they'll come up and stick their square to the chart above the color of the ingredient they think is the stickiest.

4. Go over clean up procedures. Tell the students to throw away newspaper and wipe their tables with sponges. Tell them that while some students are cleaning up, others will be sticking their squares on the graph; this way, there won't be crowding at the graph.

5. Pass out the construction paper squares, and have students begin cleaning up and adding to the graph. As students finish, give them ziplock bags, and have them store their pastes to take home later.

6. After their results are posted on the graph, ask students for their observations about the graph. Encourage them to start by making "true statements" about the data, such as, "Seven people thought flour was the stickiest ingredient," or "More people thought cornstarch was stickier than salt." Ask additional comparison and number questions about the graph as time and interest permit.

7. After the session, wash and rinse the color-dot cups and the plastic spoons, and let them air dry.

Going Further

1. Have students use their pastes to work together to make a colorful classroom collage, using magazine clippings, colored paper, or other materials.

2. Older students can make bar graphs displaying the results and make math statements using the bar graph.

Students may also attempt to state some further conclusions, such as, "Cornstarch is the ingredient that makes paste the stickiest." Validate all ideas. You may want to add that even though the graph may show that more students considered cornstarch to be the stickiest ingredient, this is only based on one activity. Other experiments would have to be done to "prove" any of their conclusions.

Paste

Is not to taste

Nor does paste

Make waste

Here's the trick:

Paste makes

Things stick!

Session 2: Tasting and Describing Cola

Overview

Two of the most fundamental processes in scientific investigation are observing things and identifying their attributes. This session is the first of three sessions in which your students will observe and compare the attributes of colas. This initial cola session begins with a guessing game to introduce the meaning of the word "attribute." Next, students focus on the attributes of cola by tasting a bit of commercial cola and brainstorming a list of its attributes. They also spend some time considering the possible ingredients of cola. At the end of the session, students use their list of attributes to make up riddles about cola.

Special Note: Be sensitive to dietary restrictions that some students may have. Several teachers have cautioned that, if you have students with food allergies or diabetes, you may need to take special measures as regards the sugar in the cola activity, possibly, for example, using artificial sweeteners. Be aware also that there are some students who are not allowed to have caffeine for health or religious reasons.

What You Need

For the class:
- ❒ 3 12-oz. cans of cold, unopened cola (all the same brand)
- ❒ 1 paper cup (3 oz.)
- ❒ a clean, clear, plastic cup for each student (approximately 8 to 10 oz.) (These are the "personal cups" and should be the same kind as the cups with the colored dots used in Session 1.)
- ❒ a dump bucket (if no sink is available)
- ❒ 1 wide-tipped, black permanent felt marker
- ❒ writing paper
- ❒ pencils
- ❒ a chalkboard or a large piece of butcher paper to list attributes
- ❒ (*optional*) crayons (for students to draw images of attributes with their riddles)

Getting Ready

Prepare the cola. Refrigerate the cans of cola.

 ## Telling Attribute Riddles

1. Tell the class that you are going to play a guessing game. Say that you're thinking of something people can drink, and you'll give them hints until they guess what it is. Ask them to listen carefully to each hint you give, and raise their hands if they have a guess.

2. Pick a familiar drink like hot chocolate for them to guess. Give hints, one at a time, asking for a student to make a guess after each hint. Possible hints for hot chocolate are: It's brown, not see-through, hot, sweet, and "chocolate-y." Continue until someone guesses hot chocolate.

3. Play once or twice more if time and interest allow. Tell them that they're great guessers, and that all the hints you gave are *attributes* of the drinks. Attributes tell what something is like.

4. Explain that you can make a riddle using attributes. Ask students to think of three attributes of grape juice. Write the attributes on the board in the form of a riddle: "What's purple, good for you, and comes from a fruit that's the size of a marble?" [Grape juice!]

5. Continue creating "riddles" about one or two other familiar drinks, but don't make any riddles about cola yet.

Tasting and Describing Cola

1. Tell the class that they will soon be working on secret formulas for another drink...cola! Today they will begin by tasting a *little* bit of real cola, to help them think of attributes of a good cola.

2. Pass out the personal cups. Open the cans of cola and pour each child about half an inch of cold cola. Before tasting, have students use their other senses—sight, hearing, and smell. Then have students take little sips, while you ask them for attributes of cola. [fizzy, foamy, bubbly, brown, sweet, tasty, cold, good, not thick]

You may want to have a "riddle book" on hand to provide students with some examples of riddles, or have several such books on hand for students to read and enjoy.

3. Write a list of these words on a piece of butcher paper or on the chalkboard, and entitle it "Attributes of Cola." (Save this list for Session 4.) If the students don't mention sweetness, prompt them by asking, "Would you like sour cola?"

4. Along with attributes, students will probably contribute ideas about what ingredients they think are in cola. [carbon dioxide, caffeine, air, sugar, etc.] If this happens, list those separately, but entitle the list "Ingredients?"

5. Ask students to finish their colas or to pour leftover cola out in a dump bucket or sink. Collect their empty cups, and have students return to their seats.

Writing a Cola Attribute Riddle

1. Tell the students that they will each get to write a riddle about cola to ask their parents or friends to solve. When they solve the riddle, their parents will find out what their next secret formula project will be.

2. Explain that they should pick three attributes from the list on the board, or any other attributes of cola that they think of, to make a riddle. To make sure they get the idea, have the class work on one or two cola riddles together, pointing out that a good riddle lists all real attributes, but is still tricky to guess. Here's an example: "What's sweet, popular, and goes to a lot of parties?" [Cola!]

3. Have the students write their own riddle (or more than one, if they have time) and then take them home to try on their parents and/or siblings. Encourage them to share their riddles with their teammates and help each other as necessary. They may want to draw a picture showing attributes to go with their riddles.

*Common ingredients in many colas include water, sugar or artificial sweeteners, carbon dioxide gas for bubbles, coloring, caffeine, and flavorings. Cola companies keep some of their ingredients secret so no one will copy them. They also list ingredients in various ways. Some companies disclose the **kind** of ingredients they use, but not their exact nature. For example, some companies list "flavorings," without being specific. Companies also may disclose all or most ingredients, but keep the exact **amounts** of the ingredients (as well as their cooking, mixing, or other manufacturing processes) secret. See the "Behind the Scenes" and "Resources" sections for more information.*

The GEMS guides Liquid Explorations *and* Frog Math *also emphasize observation and understanding of attributes.* Frog and Toad Are Friends, *used in the* Frog Math *activities, is a nice literature connection for all of these attribute activities.*

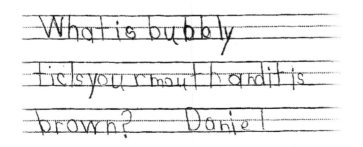

Going Further

1. Students could make a class or school graph of their favorite brands of cola or all soft drinks. The bar graph could be made from cut out pictures of little cola cans. Students could start by brainstorming a list of the colas they've tasted, then create a preference graph of their favorites. Who would be interested in the results of this graph? Why? Students could also survey their families about their favorite colas, bring in the results, and graph them on a separate graph. How do the two graphs compare?

2. Have students bring in three favorite brands of cola and compare the ingredients that are listed by the manufacturers. In what order are the ingredients listed? How many of the ingredients are the same for each cola? How many additional ingredients are in each cola?

Session 3: Investigating an Ingredient of Cola

Overview

In the previous session, students established that one of the attributes of cola is that it is sweet. In this session, they focus on an ingredient that causes sweetness—sugar! Students explore the central concept of cause and effect, finding out for themselves that not only does sugar cause sweetness, but **the more sugar we add, the sweeter the drink will taste.**

Students first watch as you add different amounts of sugar to water in three cups. They predict which will taste the sweetest. Then you switch the cups around so they become "mystery cups." Which cup has one, three, or six spoons of sugar in it? The students get to taste the three mystery sugar waters to find out which is which.

Next, you present the class with cups of sugar water that you've previously mixed to be the same sweetness as cola. How can they find out how many spoonfuls of sugar are in it? In their personal cups, the students carefully measure sugar and mix it with water, keeping a written tally of the amount they add, until it tastes as sweet as the "cola water." This activity provides students with information about how much sugar they may want to add when they make their own secret formula for cola, while also introducing the idea of repeatability of results—**if we use the same amount of sugar and water as someone else does, the sweetness of both drinks will be the same.**

The sugar solution we chose to represent cola (the "cola water") has less sugar than real commercial colas do. It tastes about as sweet because commercial colas also have bitter and sour ingredients. We've found the amount of sugar we suggest works well for this activity.

What You Need

For the class:
- ❑ 1 pitcher, 2-qt. capacity
- ❑ a 1-tsp. measuring spoon
- ❑ 1 measuring cup
- ❑ all personal cups from Session 2, rinsed
- ❑ about 5 lbs. white, granulated sugar
- ❑ extra paper towels and sponge(s)
- ❑ 1 black permanent felt marker
- ❑ 3 unlabeled plastic cups
- ❑ 1 small, lightweight plastic spoon
- ❑ 1 plastic stirrer
- ❑ 1 popsicle stick
- ❑ a stack of newspapers to cover the desks

Activity 1: Mystery Sugar Waters gives students powerful experience with cause and effect—the more sugar, the sweeter the cola. However, if you feel that your students already have a firm grasp on that concept, and if preparation time is a big consideration, you may want to skip Activity 1 and go directly to Activity 2: Matching the Sweetness of Cola.

Reminder: *There are 8 ounces in a cup, 4 cups to a quart, and 4 quarts to a gallon.*

For each group of four students:
- ❏ 1 cafeteria tray
- ❏ all the plastic cups with colored dots from Session 1, washed
- ❏ 4 paper cups (3 oz.)
- ❏ 4 small, lightweight plastic spoons
- ❏ 4 plastic stirrers
- ❏ 4 popsicle sticks
- ❏ 1 dump container (cottage cheese-type is fine)
- ❏ 4 pieces scratch paper
- ❏ 4 pencils
- ❏ a few paper towels

Getting Ready

There are two activities in this session, Mystery Sugar Waters and Matching the Sweetness of Cola. Preparation includes mixing several sugar water solutions of different concentrations and pouring them into color-coded cups. In testing, we have found **it is most efficient to prepare for the SECOND activity first.**

Getting Ready for Activity 2: Matching the Sweetness of Cola

In this activity, students will mix sugar and water to try to match the sweetness of a "cola water" solution you've made that is as sweet as cola.

1. **Mix "cola water" for the orange-dot cups.** First, decide how many cups of cola water you need for the whole class. Figure that every **group** of students will get one cup, containing about three ounces. If you have eight groups, you need eight times three ounces, or 24 ounces of solution for the whole class. To make the cola water, mix three level **measuring** teaspoons of sugar per **8 ounces** of water in the pitcher.

2. **Fill the orange-dot cups.** Pour about three ounces of the cola water into an orange-dot cup for each group.

3. **Prepare the dry sugar cups.** Put about a half-cup of sugar into each of the two red-dot cups for each group. Place two small plastic spoons, two popsicle sticks, and two plastic stirrers in each cup.

4. **Arrange materials on trays.** Put these materials on each group's tray:

- 1 orange-dot cup of cola water
- 2 red-dot cups with sugar, spoons, popsicle sticks, and stirrers
- 4 paper cups
- 4 pieces of scratch paper
- 4 pencils

5. **Set aside the trays for later.** Put the trays aside, ready for quick distribution for the second activity in the session.

Getting Ready for Activity 1: Mystery Sugar Waters

This is the first activity in the session, in which students try to determine the sweetness of three mystery sugar waters. These Activity 1 materials do not go on the groups' trays.

1. **Prepare three other sugar water solutions.** Using the pitcher as you did for the cola water (orange-dot) solution above, mix three other sugar water solutions of varying sweetness, according to the directions below. Pour each solution into the appropriate color-coded cups, filling them each about three ounces full. Keep track of which solution you put in each color-coded cup, but don't make a color-code chart. This time it's a secret!

- For the **blue-dot** cups: Mix 1 level measuring teaspoon of sugar per cup of water in the pitcher.

- For the **yellow-dot** cups: Mix 3 level measuring teaspoons of sugar per cup of water in the pitcher. (You might notice that this is the same concentration as the cola water solution in Activity 2—that's fine!)

- For the **green-dot** cups: Mix 6 level measuring teaspoons of sugar per cup of water in the pitcher.

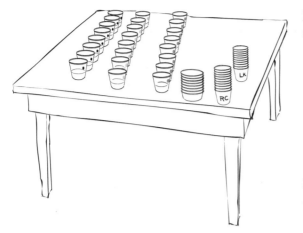

2. **Assemble the materials.** Have the Activity 1 materials all in one place, ready for distribution, but not on trays:

- all of the blue-, yellow-, and green-dot cups of solutions (with about three ounces in each cup)

- students' personal cups

- 1 dump container for each group

3. Have handy near where you will introduce the activities:

- three unlabeled plastic cups, each with three ounces of plain water

- a cup half-full of sugar with a small plastic spoon, a popsicle stick, and stirrer

- a pitcher of plain water

The First Activity: Mystery Sugar Waters

Introducing the Activity

1. Point to your three demonstration cups of water and the cup of sugar. Say that one of the ingredients that is in most colas is sugar. Tell students they'll get to do two sugar-tasting activities in this class session that might help them decide how much sugar they want to put in their own cola formulas later.

2. Say that you're going to put some sugar into the cups of water and stir. Ask for predictions about what will happen. [water will get sweet, sugar will dissolve, sugar might swirl around, sugar won't go on the bottom] Accept all answers.

3. Explain that you're going to put **one** level spoonful of sugar into the first cup, **three** spoonfuls into the second, and **six** into the third. Demonstrate how to flatten the sugar with the popsicle stick, and use the plastic stirrer to mix the liquid. As you measure and mix, ask, "If you tasted these, which do you think would be the sweetest?" "The least sweet?" "Why?" (Don't insist that students understand just yet that the more sugar you add the sweeter the water will taste. They will soon have an opportunity to discover this.)

Although the students' intuitive understanding of dissolving will be enhanced by this activity, the concept of dissolving is not intended to be a main focus here. Please see the GEMS unit Involving Dissolving, *in which students thoroughly explore the challenging concept that dissolved sugar is still there even though we can't see it any more.*

For the cola making activities of Sessions 3 and 4, some teachers prefer to have students level the sugar using the stirrers, and stir using the popsicle sticks in order to better dissolve the sugar.

4. Slide the cups around each other a few times on the table so that the students can no longer tell which is which. Say they are now "mystery cups." Ask, "*Now* how can we tell which mystery cup has one, three, or six spoonfuls of sugar?" [taste, look carefully]

Tasting the Mystery Sugar Waters

1. Say that you made three cups just like these for each group. Explain that they are in three different color-coded cups so students will know that they have all three mystery cups, but they won't know which is which.

2. Briefly demonstrate how a student will choose a sugar water from one of the mystery cups, pour a little sip into their personal cup, and taste. Tell them to pour out the extra, if any, into the dump container, and taste the sugar water from each of the other two mystery cups the same way. Say that it's okay to re-taste one of the sugar waters, but students should make sure not to mix them up.

3. As needed, have helpers pass out newspaper so groups can cover their desks. Have helpers pass out students' personal cups, and a dump container for each group, and carefully take the three different mystery cups to each group. Have the class begin.

4. As groups finish, collect all the materials except their personal cups (now empty) and ask, "Which cup do you think had six spoonfuls of sugar in it?" [green-dot cup] "Why?" [It tasted the sweetest.] "Which do you think was the cup with three spoonfuls of sugar?" "Why?" "One spoonful?" "What can we say about adding sugar—what effect does it cause?" [The more sugar you put in, the sweeter the water will taste.]

The Second Activity: Matching the Sweetness of Cola

Introducing the Activity

1. Reinforce the idea that the more sugar added, the sweeter the drink, by asking: "Why might one cola, like Pepsi, taste sweeter than another, say Classic Coke?" [maybe Pepsi has more sugar, maybe Classic Coke has some sour ingredients, etc.]

Cola companies do tell us how much sugar is in their colas. They don't keep that part of their formula secret, because people need to know how much sugar is in food products for health reasons.

2. Hold up an orange-dot cup, and ask, "How many spoonfuls of sugar do you think might be in this much Classic Coke?"

3. Say that you got the sugar formula for Classic Coke, and used the formula to mix this sugar water that tastes as sweet as Classic Coke!

4. Say that they will each get a sample of this "cola water" in their group's orange-dot cup. Ask, "How could your group find out how much sugar is in this cola water?" Take a few suggestions, and then explain that they will taste it, and, in their personal cup, mix spoonfuls of sugar with plain water until it matches the sweetness of the cola water. They'll need to carefully count the spoons of sugar they put in.

Explaining the Procedure

1. Say that because of germs, their group can't all taste from the same orange-dot cup, so there are little paper cups for each of them on the tray for tasting the cola water. Each student in the group needs to pour a little cola water into a paper cup.

2. They'll each get plain water in their plastic personal cup.

3. There are two red-dot cups of sugar on their group's tray. Say that kids love sugar, but during our scientific testing, it is not okay to taste the dry sugar. Remind them to level the sugar with the popsicle stick.

4. Write the word "sugar" on the chalkboard. Say that they will each write "sugar" on a piece of scratch paper. Each time they add one level spoonful to their personal cup, they make a tally mark on the paper. As needed, demonstrate how to make a tally mark.

5. After each spoonful, they'll stir their water with the stir stick until they can't see the sugar any more, taste a sip, and then taste a sip of the cola water in their paper cup. If the water in their personal cup isn't as sweet as the cola water, they do it again: measure, add, tally, stir, taste. Emphasize that they should not add any sugar to the paper cup.

6. Ask students if they think it will be hard to stop adding sugar? What will happen if they add too much? What if theirs gets sweeter than the cola water? Then they should stop, check how many spoonfuls they've added, and just don't count the last one. Tell them that you are confident that they will try to stop when their water is sweet enough, as they are gathering scientific information for making cola later. (You may want to set an upper limit for adding spoonfuls, such as no more than six.)

Experimenting and Graphing Results

1. When you are satisfied that students understand the procedure, have one student from each group come get a tray of materials. With your pitcher of water, fill all the students' personal cups to the bottom of their initials (the 3 ounce level) and have them begin.

2. Walk around and check that students are remembering to tally and taste between spoonfuls. Remind them to take small sips. To help students resist the temptation to overdo it, it's wise to take the sugar cups away from groups as they finish. Most students will stop on their own.

3. When it seems that most groups are done, ask everyone to stop. Have them put all the materials on the tray and have one student from each group take the tray to a central location.

4. Write the numbers 1 through 5 on the chalkboard (or butcher paper) horizontally along a lower edge. Quickly poll the class for the number of spoonfuls they think was needed to match the sweetness of the cola water.

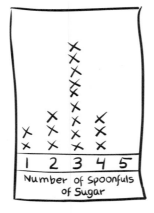

One teacher told us, "My third grade students made their comparisons in halves of spoonfuls to try to be more exact in telling me how many spoons matched the cola water."

What's the "right" number of spoonfuls? Classic Coke actually has more sugar per cup, but they also have bitter or sour ingredients that mask some of the sweetness. Our "cola water" is of course only a rough approximation.

Keep in mind that, to mix the "cola water," you used 3 teaspoon-size measuring spoons of sugar per cup of water. The students are using the lightweight plastic spoons, which are equivalent to a half teaspoon, and mixing the sugar into three ounces of water (less than half a cup). Theoretically, this means that two or three student spoonfuls of sugar are enough to match the sweetness of their orange-dot "cola water." The students' actual results will vary, which is fine. (See the concluding discussion and graphing, at left.)

*Because the students taste the solution in the personal cups after adding each spoonful of sugar, they'll have progressively less water, so they'll be adding proportionately more sugar each time. But since the students will be tasting only a sip, this is okay. Still, it's worth emphasizing that the students should take **little** sips.*

If you have a standard seating arrangement and you can set up trays to coincide with it, then it is possible for you or one of your helpers to have the personal cups on the trays and fill them with water beforehand.

With older students, you may want to encourage a brief discussion of why different students might get different results. [measuring differences, different taste buds, etc.] Scientists also obtain differing results sometimes. What could scientists do when they get different results? [do experiments over again, design new experiments, etc.]

5. Ask, "How many think it took one spoonful?" Count those students and make a column of Xs above the number 1 on the board to create a quick bar graph. Continue making Xs until you've recorded all students' responses. Ask the class to look at the graph to summarize how many spoonfuls most people decided matched the cola water. Save the graph for Session 4.

6. Save the two red-dot cups of sugar with spoons, popsicle sticks, and stirrers for Session 4.

7. Pour out all sugar waters. Throw away paper cups. Wash and rinse plastic cups and stack them to dry. Have the students wipe off tables if necessary.

What is the cause

Of the sweetness of drink?

Where does it come from—

What do you think?

It comes from the sugar

Let me tell you—

The more spoonfuls of sugar

The sweeter the brew.

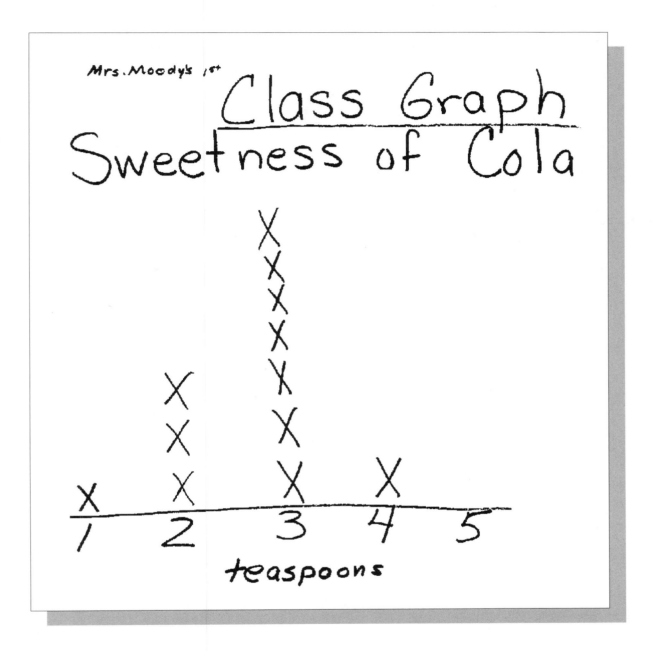

Session 4: Secret Formulas for Cola

Overview

In this session, students apply what they learned in the previous session about optimum amounts of sugar, and also add other ingredients to make their personal secret formula for cola. This time, they record their secret formula on a data sheet.

Students start with club soda, to which you add brown food coloring. They then choose from four additional ingredients: sugar, vanilla, cinnamon, and lime juice. Students use measuring, recording, and testing skills. When their colas are complete, students add ice cubes, and enjoy.

The final discussion centers on whether their cola would come out exactly the same if they used their secret formula again. If they change an ingredient or an amount, will the cola be different? The concept that results are repeatable (if we follow the same exact procedure, the same result will happen) may not yet be obvious to students. This is all right. You may find that they gain understanding of this important concept gradually, over the course of the entire *Secret Formulas* unit.

What You Need

For the class:

- ❒ 1 piece of large white construction paper to make class color key
- ❒ the list of cola attributes from Session 2
- ❒ the class graph of sugar amounts from Session 3
- ❒ a few colored dots in the colors used previously
- ❒ 1 wide-tipped, felt black marker
- ❒ 1 bag ice cubes (at least 1 cube per student)
- ❒ 1 teaspoon red food coloring
- ❒ $1/2$ teaspoon green food coloring
- ❒ 2 bottles lime juice (8 oz. each)
- ❒ 2 bottles vanilla extract (8 oz. each—imitation vanilla is fine)
- ❒ 1 small container ground cinnamon (containers usually have about an ounce or a little less)
- ❒ 1 lb. sugar

❒ 3 or 4 cans club soda or salt-free, flavorless seltzer water* for demonstration and as extra for class
❒ 2 plastic cups (one with teacher's initials on it)
❒ 1 dump bucket (if no sink is available)
❒ the students' personal plastic cups
❒ (optional) 1 cooler for the ice cubes
❒ (optional) 1 roll of plastic wrap (to cover vanilla extract if you need to pour it ahead of time)

*12 ounce cans of club soda are ideal because you'll be distributing one to each group of four students, who will then pour about three ounces into each of their personal cups. However, if you can't find cans, club soda is also sold in six-packs of small bottles, or large 2-liter bottles.

For each group of four students:

❒ 1 cafeteria tray
❒ 2 red-dot cups of sugar with spoons, popsicle sticks, and stirrers (from Session 3)
❒ 3 color-coded plastic cups emptied and rinsed from previous activities (one each of blue, green, and yellow)
❒ 2 flat toothpicks for cinnamon scoops
❒ 32 half-straws for droppers
❒ 1 can club soda or salt-free, flavorless seltzer water *
❒ 4 Cola data sheets (master on page 51)
❒ 4 pencils
❒ tally sheet from Session 3
❒ 1 container (cottage cheese-type) for ice
❒ (optional) crayons or markers (4 sets of red, blue, yellow, and green)

Getting Ready

1. **Make a class color key.** List sugar, lime juice, vanilla, and cinnamon on large white paper, using a marker. Next to each ingredient, put a colored dot to correspond with the cups listed in number 6, below.

2. **Make the brown food coloring.** Mix up brown food coloring in a cup. Mix 1 teaspoon red with a half teaspoon green. You'll use this at the beginning of the activity to color club soda.

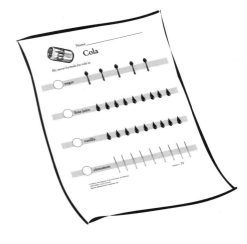

3. **Prepare the ice.** Have a bag of ice on hand. Break up the ice in the bag if it is frozen solid. If possible, keep the ice in a cooler until the end of the session.

4. **Replenish the sugar.** Add sugar to the red-dot cups so that there is about half a cup of sugar in each. Leave the two spoons, two popsicle sticks, and two stirrers in each cup.

5. **Make straw droppers.** Cut straws in half to make four straw droppers for each group plus one for you, the teacher, to use with the brown food coloring.

6. **Set up ingredients on trays.** Put ingredients into color-coded cups for each group of students, and place cups and club soda on each group's tray as follows:

- red-dot cups: Use the two red-dot cups of **sugar** with spoons, popsicle sticks, and stirrers that you saved from Session 3

- green-dot cup: Put in about $1/4$ cup of **lime juice** (2 ounces) with two droppers

- yellow-dot cup: Put in about $1/4$ cup of **vanilla** (2 ounces) with two droppers

- blue-dot cup: Put in one teaspoon **cinnamon** with two toothpicks to be used as scoops

- 1 unopened can of club soda (12 ounces)

7. **Arrange additional materials.** Have handy—but not on trays—ice, one small container per team in which to put the ice, your personal cup with initials for demonstration, and all the students' personal cups.

8. **Prepare the student data sheets.** Duplicate one Cola data sheet per student (master on page 51). If your students are non-readers and will need to color-code the ingredients on their data sheets, have red, blue, yellow, and green crayons or markers handy.

Try to pour vanilla just before the activity to minimize evaporation. If you have to pre-pour, place a piece of plastic wrap over vanilla cups to slow evaporation.

Color coding data sheets helps make identification of ingredients easier for students, especially for non-readers. Before the activity, the students can color code the data sheets with a crayon or marker to match your chart. For older students, it may not be necessary to color code data sheets.

Introducing the Ingredients

1. Ask the class to think back to when they made paste. What were the attributes of the paste? [sticky, gooey, etc.] What ingredients worked the best? Which powders did they use? How many spoonfuls of each ingredient did they use? How many squirts of water? Did they write it down? [no] Why is it important to write down formulas?

2. Tell students that they are now going to make their own secret formula for cola. This time, they will carefully record how much of each ingredient they use. If it turns out great, they will be able to make it again, exactly as great! If it turns out not so good, they can look at exactly what they put in and change the formula.

3. Introduce the new ingredients, using the class color key and holding up cups of ingredients from a tray.

4. It is helpful if students have an idea how the ingredients will taste. However, don't give them too much information about the ingredients, as students will be deciding for themselves what to add.

> a. Ask, "Have you ever tasted a lemon?" "How does it taste?" [sour!] Lime juice is like lemon juice. Ask, "What will happen to the taste of your cola if you add too much lime juice?" [very sour]

> b. Suggest that if they don't know how vanilla or cinnamon taste, they can smell them carefully, using the method of wafting. Show the class this method—bringing a smell to your nose through the air by using your hand.

> c. Ask what will happen if they use too much cinnamon. [The cola will taste more "cinnamon-y"] Stress that cinnamon is a strong spice so they should use only little toothpick scoops. Demonstrate how to tilt the cup a little, and scoop a little bit of cinnamon out on the flat end of the toothpick. Say that they will use the straw droppers to add the lime juice and vanilla—one drop at a time.

5. Refer to the class graph of how much sugar was in the cola water in Session 3, and mention that this information might be helpful in determining how much sugar to add to their own colas.

Demonstrating How to Make Your Own Cola

1. Point to the bottom of the letters marking your initials on your personal cup. Explain that each group will get one can of club soda to share, and each student will pour club soda into their cup until it touches the bottom of the letters. Add club soda to your personal cup. Mention that the bubbles are already in it and that it is clear.

2. Add a few drops of brown food coloring to your cup. Explain that you will add brown coloring to the cans of club soda for students at each table before they pour it.

One teacher suggested that a nice addition is to bring in dry ice and show students how to make soda water. This can be done by simply placing a small piece of dry ice into a cup of water.

3. Model adding and recording different ingredients. Explain that first they will add an ingredient and then record how much of it they added. Say that this time they will use their droppers to add **drops,** instead of squirts, of the vanilla and/or lime juice. Show how to squeeze the dropper gently to create drops. Encourage students to practice making drops in the lime juice or vanilla cup first if they want to further perfect their technique before creating their secret cola formulas.

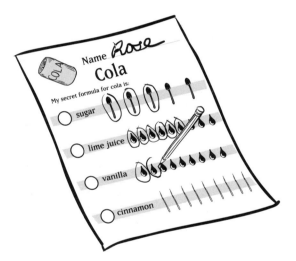

4. Model how to record the amount of each ingredient added by circling the spoons, toothpicks, or drops pictured on the Cola data sheet. Ask why it's important to record what they put into the mixture. Point out that the sheet has only nine toothpick pictures for cinnamon because that is the **most** they can use.

Drops will tend to be more uniform if the dropper is held vertically.

5. Ask students if they can take out some lime juice if they put too much in? [no!] Emphasize that they should add little amounts at a time then taste the result. Let them know that they can, if they wish, decide not to use all the ingredients.

6. Encourage them to take little tastes. When they think their cola is perfect, they should raise their hands and you will bring ice to their group. They may then add an ice cube to their cola.

Some teachers let students add ice as they make their cola.

7. (*Optional*) Color code the data sheet. If your students are not readers, they need to color code their data sheets. Have them do this now, using the class color key as a reference. Have them color in the circle by the word "sugar" red, etc.

Let the Cola Making Begin!

1. Pass out trays of materials and data sheets to students, while two or three helpers pass out the personal cups. Add about 10 drops of food coloring to each group's can of club soda as you open it. Have students begin when they have all their materials.

2. Fill up containers with four to eight ice cubes each and distribute them to the tables when students think they have made their own unique versions of "the real thing."

3. When it's time to clean up, show students where to dump cola they don't like and where to put dirty cups for washing. Collect trays of materials. Have them keep their Cola data sheets.

Discussing the Attributes of a Good Cola

1. Refer to the list of the attributes of commercial cola brainstormed during Session 2. Help students compare their colas to commercial colas by reading each word as students give a silent thumbs up/thumbs down (yes/no) response about their own cola. "Was your cola sweet?" "Brown?" "Bubbly?" "Refreshing?"

2. Ask students for their ideas about making the same cola again. Ask, "If you were to follow your formula exactly again, do you think your cola would turn out the same way?"

3. Ask, "Are there any ingredients or amounts you would choose to change for next time?"

4. Explain to students that all of the ingredients they used are easy to get at a grocery store and that their secret formula can be made again at home. They can change their cola by changing the ingredients or the amounts of ingredients in their formulas. (The data sheet doesn't include club soda or brown food coloring, so you should mention those ingredients as well.)

Going Further

1. Have your students design an advertisement for a cola. They could draw the cola can, invent a name, list ingredients, and write attributes of the cola (delicious, sparkling, tasty, sweet, etc.). Encourage them to use the data they collected during the activity to strengthen their advertisement. Invite them to explain what caused their cola to have the attributes it does. They could also write a slogan for their cola or a little advertising jingle to a familiar tune.

2. Homemade Lemonade: Give students the homework assignment of preparing their own lemonade at home. Spend time beforehand listing possible ingredients (sugar, lemons, water). You may choose to assign students a specified amount of water to begin with so their formulas are easy to compare. Ask students to record their formulas at home and bring the recipes back to school to share.

3. Making Brown: Students practice mixing primary colors to make brown. Begin with a styrofoam egg carton (or small reaction tray) and four cups filled with a bit of red, blue, green, and yellow food coloring. Instruct students to use small paint brushes to test color combinations in their egg carton dips. A data sheet showing how they filled in their choices (☐ + ☐ = ☐) might be helpful for students to keep track of which combinations they try.

4. Shopping for Cola: Compare costs of different cola brands. Agree upon a container size for a price survey (liters, six-packs, one 12-ounce can, etc.). On a shopping trip, have students record names and prices of different colas sold. Put a star next to any brand being sold at a sale price. Refer to the class graph of favorite colas. What is the cost of the favorite brand? Is there a range in price? Why might that be? Refer to the ingredients. Are there more costly ingredients in more expensive colas? What other factors might account for price differences? What brand(s) are the least expensive? The most expensive? Does the price of one brand vary depending upon where it is sold? How many brands of cola were on sale? Was a cola on sale at all the stores?

As students create and record their secret formulas for cola, they are doing a form of informal algebra (or generalized arithmetic). The equation that they all are working with could be expressed as:

___ sugar + ___ lime juice + ___ vanilla + ___ cinnamon = flavoring for cola recipe

The variables are the quantities of each ingredient they may add. As in the case of many algebraic equations, there are multiple solutions! In this case, students seek the optimal amount of each ingredient, based on their taste preferences. When the class shares their recipes, they can see if there are any common amounts for the various ingredients.

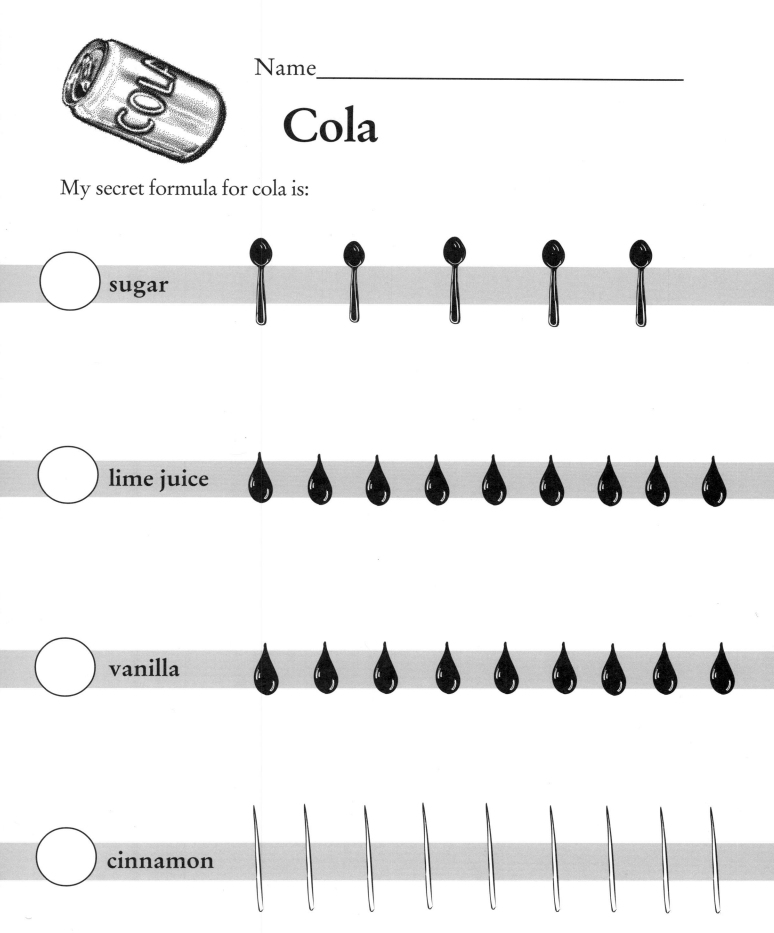

Name_____

Cola

My secret formula for cola is:

sugar

lime juice

vanilla

cinnamon

What is Like Some   Tom
Cream in an oreo cookie
Minty. Its Like a
fire ball and I tastes
Like cinnamon?

What Looks White and
Smells minty and
tastes hot and
Feels Sticky?

What Feels sticky and and
taste like thin mints
and fokes Like shaving cream
and smells minty.
Kayleigh

What looks like shaving cream
and smells like mints
and taste like pepper mint
and feels like slime?

Session 5: Tasting, Describing, and Testing Toothpaste

Overview

After the last three sessions on cola, your students now spend the next three sessions investigating toothpaste (fortunately for their teeth!). In this first toothpaste session, the students taste a small sample of commercial toothpaste, generate a list of toothpaste attributes, and make riddles using the attributes. As in the first cola session, the goal is for students to use descriptive language and practice fundamental science processes such as observing, communicating, and comparing.

Also in this session, your class begins testing four ingredients of toothpaste. Students observe the "feel" (consistency) of each ingredient in a plastic bag. In a second test, they add water to their bags and shake them to find out which ingredient makes the most foam. In Session 6, they will do one more test, to see which ingredient scrubs the best. The ingredient tests in Sessions 5 and 6 prepare your scientists well for inventing their own toothpastes in Session 7.

What You Need

For the class:

- ❐ one small tube of toothpaste, any common brand (something not too strong tasting, not one students might think "stings," and not one made with baking soda)
- ❐ 32 flat toothpicks
- ❐ paper towels
- ❐ writing paper
- ❐ pencils
- ❐ a chalkboard or butcher paper
- ❐ 1 piece of large white construction paper
- ❐ about 8 extra stick-on dots in each of these colors: yellow, green, blue, and orange
- ❐ about 100 TUMS tablets—regular flavor and color, *or* about 12 teaspoons (close to one cup) of food grade calcium carbonate powder (about half is needed for the tests in this session, and the other half for the cleaning test in Session 6)
- ❐ 1 to 2 cups Ivory Snow laundry soap
- ❐ 1 1/2 cups glycerin
- ❐ 1 1/2 cups water
- ❐ a few extra ziplock sandwich bags to replace ones that leak

Some teachers use the study of cola and toothpaste in Secret Formulas *to launch a unit about health, especially dental health. Starting with the fact that cola may not be the best of all possible "leisure beverages" for our teeth, students can learn more about nutrition, brushing and flossing their teeth, and the importance of regular check-ups.*

Note: Teachers of younger students may want to make Session 5 into two short sessions, breaking after tasting toothpaste and making riddles, then testing ingredients at a different time. If you choose to postpone the ingredient testing, follow only step 7 in the "Getting Ready" section.

The Toothpaste Millionaire *is a great story to read to your class during the course of the toothpaste activities. See the "Literature Connections" section for more details.*

Some teachers like to have two different toothpastes to sample, in different colors, etc., so students can compare attributes.

For each group of four students:

- ❒ 1 cafeteria tray
- ❒ 4 color-dot plastic cups from previous sessions: yellow, green, blue, and orange
- ❒ 4 extra plastic cups (to set bags in for stability). You can use students' personal cups or any extra cups.
- ❒ 2 droppers
- ❒ 2 small, lightweight plastic spoons
- ❒ 2 popsicle sticks
- ❒ 4 ziplock sandwich bags
- ❒ 1 paper cup (3 oz.)
- ❒ 1 container (cottage cheese-type)

Getting Ready

Before the Day of the Activity

Decide if you will be grinding up TUMS tablets or ordering food grade calcium carbonate.

Ordering Calcium Carbonate

See the "Sources for Materials" section on page 114 for information on how to order food grade calcium carbonate. The one pound container should be sufficient for a class of 32 students. Order more if you have a larger class or will be presenting to multiple classes. Calcium carbonate is needed in all three toothpaste sessions. We estimate that a total of 3 cups of powdered calcium carbonate will be more than sufficient for even a large-size class, for all three sessions, even allowing for minor spills. **Be sure to read the information on calcium carbonate in "Behind the Scenes" on page 106, including the safety note about calcium carbonate dust.**

Grinding Up TUMS

Because the main ingredient in TUMS is calcium carbonate, TUMS is also a very accessible and inexpensive source. Unfortunately, the tablets need to be ground up! (Some people have suggested using baking soda instead of calcium carbonate as the main powder ingredient in toothpaste. Baking soda is easy to get, and makes a good paste, but its taste is quite vehemently disliked by many students!)

If you will be grinding the TUMS tablets, we recommend that you or an adult volunteer do the grinding, rather than the students. This way, students won't mistakenly think that toothpaste is made from TUMS! You'll need to crush or grind about 300 total TUMS tablets for the three toothpaste sessions. Plan to set aside about two-thirds of the TUMS for use in the last of the three sessions. The grinding can be done in a number of different ways: you can use a mortar and pestle; grind the tablets in a clean coffee grinder or food blender; or put them in a ziplock bag, cover with a towel, and crush with a rolling pin or a hammer. The TUMS should be ground until roughly the consistency of corn meal or coarse ground pepper—it is not necessary to grind to a fine powder.

A note on TUMS safety: If a child were to ingest a handful of TUMS (say 20) the medical advice would be to give water or milk and watch the child for an hour as this could cause an upset stomach. Since your students will be using much smaller quantities, there is no danger; even if one of your students did choose to eat their toothpaste (rather than brushing with it) they would be eating what amounts to only three TUMS tablets.

The ziplock bag in which you grind the TUMS may get tiny holes in it during grinding; if you're going to store the ground TUMS, you may want to put the powder in another bag.

On the Day of the Activity

1. **Make a class color key.** As in previous sessions, list the ingredients on a piece of large white construction paper and stick the appropriate colored dot next to each. You won't need the red cups in this session. Keep the color key handy in the area where you will introduce the ingredients.

- orange: calcium carbonate

- yellow: soap

- green: glycerin

- blue: water

2. **Put ingredients on trays.** Put ingredients into cups for each group of students, and place on trays as follows:

- orange-dot cup: 2–3 tablespoons of calcium carbonate powder (ground TUMS)

- yellow-dot cup: about $1/8$ cup Ivory Snow soap (one ounce)

- green-dot cup: about $1/4$ cup glycerin (two ounces)

- blue-dot cup: about $1/4$ cup water (two ounces)

3. **Add droppers, spoons, and popsicle sticks.** Put one dropper into each cup of water and glycerin. Put a plastic spoon and a popsicle stick into each cup of soap and calcium carbonate.

4. **Add four extra plastic cups to trays.** These will be used in the foam activity to stabilize the bags while students add water.

5. **Color code the ziplock bags.** Stick a colored dot on one side of enough bags so that each group will have one bag of each color. Make a stack of four different-colored bags for each group.

6. **Prepare containers of water.** For each group, fill a container with water and put a three-ounce paper cup in it to serve as a measurer/dipper.

7. **Prepare dabs of commercial toothpaste.** Squeeze a small dab (about a quarter inch) of commercial toothpaste onto a paper towel for each group of four students. Have these ready to distribute, along with toothpicks, but **not on the trays.**

If you prepare for this activity well in advance of presenting it, you may want to set the paper cup beside the water container, rather than in it, to prevent it from becoming too soggy.

Introducing Toothpaste

1. Announce that in the next few class sessions, the students are going to be scientists working on a new secret formula... toothpaste! Say that you have brought some store-bought toothpaste. They'll get to taste a little bit of toothpaste today and think about attributes. Emphasize that they will only taste a tiny bit, since toothpaste is not a food. Another time, they'll do scientific tests on toothpaste ingredients, and, finally, they'll use what they have learned to make their own, personal secret formulas for toothpaste.

2. Discuss toothpaste for a few minutes by asking, "Why do people brush their teeth?" "Why is it very important to brush your teeth after drinking cola?" [sugar can cause cavities—by brushing, you help your teeth stay healthy] "When you brush, what does the brush do?" [gets food— or cola!—off your teeth]

3. Tell them that each group will get a small dab of toothpaste on a paper towel. Demonstrate how each student will use a toothpick to pick up one little bit of toothpaste to taste.

Tasting Toothpaste and Thinking of Attributes

1. Pass out the dabs of toothpaste and toothpicks. Ask the students to think of attributes of toothpaste as they look at, smell, and taste it.

2. After a few minutes, regain the attention of the class, and ask them for some attributes of toothpaste. [white, thick, shiny, gooshy, smells good, tastes minty] List the attributes on a piece of butcher paper or on a part of the chalkboard that can be saved during the next few class sessions. Include in the list any general attributes of toothpaste that they've heard about or know from brushing their teeth [gets bacteria off, makes lots of foam, makes teeth sparkle, comes in different colors, gels, tubes or pumps, etc.] Entitle the list: "Attributes of Toothpaste."

3. If no one mentions ingredients, ask the class what they think some of the ingredients of toothpaste might be, and accept all their ideas. Tell them they will find out more about the ingredients of toothpaste later on.

4. Collect and throw away the toothpicks and dabs of toothpaste.

Making Attribute Riddles for Toothpaste

1. Tell the students that they will each get to write a riddle about toothpaste using attributes, just as they did with cola.

2. Remind them that they can use three attributes from the list on the board, or use any other attributes of toothpaste that they think of. Have the class work on one or two toothpaste riddles together (such as, "What's pasty, foamy, and makes your smile sparkle?")

3. Have the students spend a few minutes writing their own riddle (or more than one, if they have time), and then take them home to try on their parents and/or siblings. Encourage them to share their riddles with their teammates and help each other as necessary.

Note: If you have decided to make this session into two shorter sessions, end the first part here.

Introducing Four Toothpaste Ingredients

Don't feel you need to tell the students too much now about glycerin and calcium carbonate. One goal of this session is for the students themselves to observe the attributes of the ingredients. If they find it hard to pronounce these words, they can refer to them by their color code for now.

1. Regain the attention of the class. Using a tray of materials, briefly introduce each cup of toothpaste ingredients, referring to the class color key. Mention that glycerin and calcium carbonate are ingredients often used in making toothpaste; glycerin looks like water but is thicker; calcium carbonate is a powder.

2. Be sure to emphasize to your students that although these are all safe ingredients for making toothpaste, **they are not food. Stress that today students are NOT going to taste these ingredients at all.**

Introducing the Feel Test

With older students, you might want to use the words "texture" and "consistency."

1. Say that now they'll get to do two tests that may help them decide later which ingredients to put in their secret formulas for toothpaste. Ask, "What does toothpaste feel like when you touch it?" "Is it squishy?" "What are some words that describe how it feels?"

2. Demonstrate how each person in their group will add one of the four test ingredients to a plastic bag. (Partners will hold the bag while the ingredients are being added.) The color dot on their bag should match the ingredient they test.

3. Write the amounts they should use on the board, perhaps drawing symbols of four droppers or a spoon plus two droppers. Explain that the water added to the two powders is so that students can test how they feel when they are wet.

- 4 dropper squirts for glycerin

- 4 dropper squirts for water

- 1 level spoonful for calcium carbonate, plus 2 dropper squirts of water

- 1 level spoonful for soap, plus 2 dropper squirts of water

4. Remind students to level their powders with the popsicle sticks. As you demonstrate adding one of the ingredients to a bag, show how to feel the ingredient through the bag.

5. Ask them to notice what the ingredients feel like, especially which are more watery or slimy and which are thicker and drier.

If your ground TUMS has some chunks in it, be aware that they can poke holes in the plastic bag if squeezed too hard. Later, when the students add water for the foam test, the bags may leak. Ask students to feel the calcium carbonate gently.

Introducing the Foam Test

1. Say that before they get their materials, you need to explain one more test they get to do. Ask for thumbs up if they like foamy, bubbly toothpaste, thumbs down if they don't, and thumbs sideways if they like it just a little foamy. Say that they'll get to add more water to their bags and shake them to see how foamy it gets.

2. Demonstrate how to add water to their ziplock bag. Dip a paper cup into a container of water (half a cup is fine) and pour the water into the bag with one of the ingredients already in it. (The student who has the bag with water just adds more water—that is her ingredient.)

3. Show how to set the bag into a cup for stability, and zip up the bag. When they think their bag is zipped, they should raise their hand, and you will come and check their seal. Then they shake their bag. After shaking, they will set the bags in cups next to each other and see which ingredient made the most foam. Tell them to be sure that everyone in their group gets to see how foamy each ingredient gets.

Doing the Feel and Foam Tests

1. Quickly remind them of the two procedures: FIRST add an ingredient to a bag and do a feel test, THEN add a paper cup of water, zip, and shake for the foam test. Have one student from each group come up and get a tray of materials. Have groups begin.

2. When students add water for the foam test, go around and check the seals on their bags. Have the extra plastic bags handy in case some bags spring leaks. When everyone has had a chance to shake and observe their bags for foaminess, have students take trays and bags back to a central area. Have them wipe tables as necessary.

Some teachers prefer to conduct and debrief these two tests separately. The students would first do the feel test, then discuss the results. Then students do the foam test and discuss its results.

Discussing the Results of the Tests

1. Regain the attention of the class. Tape the color key of ingredients on the chalkboard, and write the heading "Foam Test" next to it. Collect opinions from a reporter at each table about which ingredient made the most foam, and record it on the board by putting stars next to the names of the ingredients. Summarize the class results by asking, "If you like foamy toothpaste, which ingredient(s) would be good to include?"

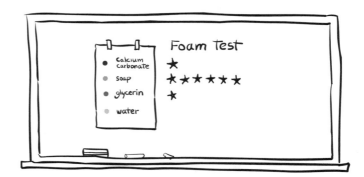

2. Ask the class to think back to how each ingredient felt *before* they poured in the cup of water for the foam test. Accept several responses for each ingredient.

Clean Up

1. Save the trays of ingredient cups for the next two sessions. You may want to stack the trays to save space. If your ingredient cups are low on calcium carbonate, allow time to grind some more for the next two sessions.

2. Leave the foam test results on the chalkboard for Session 6.

3. Empty water containers, and discard the ziplock bags and paper cups. (If you wish, you can, after dumping the water, save the bags that **had only water in them** for re-use in Session 8.)

4. Save the color-key list of ingredients for Sessions 6 and 7.

Going Further

1. One teacher who tested this unit had her second graders write riddles using the letters in toothpaste. See one of their imaginative creations on this page.

2. The "tooth in cola trick" is an interesting extension to this session, and relates to both cola and toothpaste. Place a tooth in a glass of cola. Observe what happens over time. Students can keep journals to record their observations. In the "trick," the cola eats the tooth away due to cola's acidity. This simulates *part* of the process that happens in our mouths when tooth decay occurs. It is not, however, an exact representation of what goes on because actual tooth decay also involves bacteria. In the actual process, mouth bacteria, nourished by sugar, produce acid, which makes holes in teeth. Cola is particularly harmful for teeth, first because it contains lots of sugar that will feed the bacteria to produce acid, AND second because it is already acidic. It is the cola's own acid that dissolves the tooth in the glass. Since none of our mouth's bacteria is present in the "tooth in cola trick," it is not exactly the same—but it sure makes the point!

3. Venn Diagrams: Choose the two most popular toothpastes. List the attributes of each. Create a Venn diagram of those attributes. What attributes are common to both? [the intersection of those two sets] Now choose two very different toothpastes. List their attributes and then create a Venn diagram. Does the diagram reveal more about the differences or similarities than students might expect? Is there an intersection of the set of attributes? Why or why not? With a partner, students can choose any two toothpastes and create a Venn diagram. As they share their work, see if there is a set of attributes that is common to **all** toothpastes.

Ms Barbara McLarty's class
2nd grade
Kingman, AZ

The thing I'm looking at is so bumpy.
One smell you will think it is the best.
One taste of it you will have to have more.
The thing I've tasted is minty and tickles your tongue.
He cleans your teeth after every meal.
People think he is good for your teeth.
And he makes your teeth clean.
Some people may like me, some may not.
The teeth in your mouth love it.
Each time I tasted it it tasted better then before.

Explain to the students that while the Tooth Fairy is unwilling to part with teeth, many oral surgeons will give them out. These teeth may be used to conduct a simple demonstration. Soak one tooth each in three separate cups—one filled with cola, one with milk, and one with water. Have students observe what happens over the next few days.

Session 6: Testing More Toothpaste Ingredients

Overview

Students continue their investigation of four toothpaste ingredients, this time testing which ingredient cleans the best. In this session, students make a blueberry stain on a ceramic tile, and then use different ingredients to try to scrub it off.

In summarizing their test results from the previous session and this one, you reinforce the concept of cause and effect. Like all scientists, your students will rely on their growing understanding of cause and effect as they make their own toothpastes. For instance, having learned about the attributes of soap, they can predict what will happen if they put lots of soap in their toothpaste formulas: the effect will be that the toothpaste will be foamy and clean well, but it will also be slicker and taste bad!

What You Need

For the class:

- ❏ 1 pair of scissors
- ❏ 1 ceramic tile for your demonstration
- ❏ a stack of paper towels
- ❏ 1 tablespoon of bleach
- ❏ 4 permanent markers (one each: yellow, green, blue, and orange)
- ❏ 1 small can blueberries*
- ❏ 1 spoon for blueberries
- ❏ 1 rinse tub (a bucket or dishpan big enough to hold 32 tiles)

  *Once opened, canned blueberries will get moldy after a few days; if some of the berries need to be saved for another class, freeze them until they're needed.

For each group of four students:

- ❏ tray with cups of ingredients, and droppers, spoons, and popsicle sticks from Session 5
- ❏ 4 ceramic tiles, about 4" x 4" (The backs of the tiles are used for the activity, and need to be porous and white. The color on the front of the tiles doesn't matter.)
- ❏ 1 paper cup (any size—for blueberries)
- ❏ 2 cotton swabs
- ❏ 4 paper towels
- ❏ 1 sponge (to be cut in four pieces for scrubbing. See #2 below.)

Getting Ready

Materials on Trays

1. **Set out the trays of materials from Session 5.** Have the trays ready to distribute. Replenish the ingredient cups if necessary. Check droppers, spoons, and popsicle sticks.

2. **Add sponge pieces to trays.** Cut a sponge into four pieces for each group. Wet the sponge pieces and squeeze them out so that they will be somewhat damp for the scrubbing activity. Add four small sponge pieces to each group's tray.

One out of four sponge pieces will be used with soap, which is hard to rinse completely out of sponges. One teacher who planned to re-use materials later, with other classes, decided to get different-colored sponges and make sure one color was always used with soap. Another used four different-colored sponges to match the color scheme of the tiles.

Materials Not on Trays

1. **Color code the tiles.** Using permanent markers in the four ingredient colors (orange, yellow, green, and blue), color code enough tiles so that each group will have one of each color. To color code, make a dot of color in one corner of the **back** of the tile. The dot should be small, but easy to see. Make a stack of four different-colored tiles for each group.

2. **Prepare cups of blueberries.** Put a small spoonful of blueberries into a paper cup for each team. Add two cotton swabs to each cup.

3. **Organize blueberry cups and tiles.** Have, in one area, ready for quick distribution after your introductory demonstration: the tile stacks, the cups of blueberries, and four paper towels per group.

4. **Organize your demonstration materials.** Have an extra tile, a paper towel, a cup of blueberries, and one of the trays of ingredients handy near where you will introduce the activity.

5. **Set up a rinse station.** Fill a rinse tub half-full of water and put it in a central location. Set a small pile of paper towels next to it. If you have a sink, it could serve as a second rinse station.

Introducing the Cleaning Test

1. Briefly review their findings from the feel and foam tests of Session 5. Help students think about cause and effect by asking what toothpaste would be like with too much or too little of a given ingredient. "If you hate dry toothpaste, what should you add?" [water or glycerin] "If you love foamy toothpaste, what should you add?" [soap]

2. Remind the class that one important attribute of toothpaste is that it cleans teeth. Today, they will test the same four ingredients to see which one cleans the best.

3. Ask students how they could find out which ingredient cleans the best. After they have shared a few ideas, hold up a tile, and tell students that instead of taking a tooth out of their mouths on which to test the ingredients, they will be using tiles as "pretend" teeth. They'll stain the **back** of the tiles, then they'll try each ingredient to see which scrubs it clean the best.

Staining the Tiles

1. Say that one food that can really stain teeth is blueberries. Explain that everyone will make a stain on a tile with blueberries. Tell the students not to taste the blueberries.

2. Show students how to set their tile on a paper towel with the shiny side down. Explain that they will put a stain on the **back** of the tile, in the middle.

3. Demonstrate how to dip a cotton swab into the blueberries and use it to make a stain about as big as a quarter on the middle of the back of your demonstration tile. Tell students to be careful because blueberries also can make stains on clothes and fingers. (Although the stain does not stay on fingers forever, it may not come out of their clothes.) Also mention that the tiles are breakable.

One teacher used a purple water-based marker instead of blueberries to make the stains on the tiles. Students marked their own tiles with a small purple dot, then used each ingredient in turn (soap last) to scrub it. They rinsed their sponges in between ingredients (so access to a rinse tub or sink is needed). Their data sheet showed each ingredient, followed by smiling face, straight face, and sad face categories. If you decide to use marker for the stains, be sure to test and scrub some samples yourself first.

Depending on your tiles, you may find that there is a square or diamond shape on the back that could be used as a boundary.

Tile with shiny side down

4. Pass out the blueberries, paper towels, and a stack of four tiles to each group, but don't pass out the trays of materials yet. Have students begin making their stains. As each group finishes, collect their cup of blueberries and cotton swabs.

Explaining the Procedure for the Cleaning Test

1. Regain the attention of the class. Explain that each student in their group will put one of the four ingredients on their tile. The colored dot in the corner of their tile will tell them which ingredient they will put on. Make sure they understand by asking, "If you have a tile with a blue dot on it, which ingredient will you use?" [water] and so on. Tell them that later they will trade tiles, and everyone will get to scrub all four.

2. Use the materials to demonstrate as you explain how to measure the ingredients. (To help students remember these amounts, you may want to write "wet" on the board and draw two droppers after it, then "dry" with a drawing of a spoon.)

- If their ingredient is **wet** (glycerin or water) they will squirt **two dropperfuls** onto the stain.

- If their ingredient is **dry** (calcium carbonate or soap) they will put **one level spoonful** on the stain.

3. Because some students may think the goal is simply to scrub all the tiles clean, remind them of the real goal by asking, "What are we trying to find out?" [which ingredient cleans best] Ask, "What if some of the stains *don't* come off?" [That will be fine, because then we'll know which ingredients don't clean as well.]

4. Explain that they'll pass the tiles around in their group for the scrubbing. When you give the signal, everyone will scrub the tile they have now, while you count to 10. Then everyone will pass that tile to the person on their right. (Have everyone raise their right hand and see who is sitting on that side of them.) **Tell them that they should pass the sponges along with the tiles, so the soapy sponge stays with the soapy tile, etc.** Everyone will scrub for another count of 10, then they'll pass that tile to the right, and so on, until they get their starting tile back.

Some teachers may prefer not to have the tiles passed around, but instead have each student scrub the tile they have for a longer period and compare results. While this may be a more simple procedure logistically, it doesn't allow all students the chance to test all four ingredients themselves.

5. Tell the students not to start scrubbing until your signal. (Any signal you normally use to get the attention of the class, such as flicking the lights, is fine.)

Conducting the Cleaning Test

1. Pass out the trays of materials, and have the students put ingredients on their tiles.

2. Give your signal to start, and count to 10 as they scrub, and then ask students to pass their tiles and sponges to the right. Repeat this process of counting-scrubbing-passing three more times.

3. Have the class stop and put their sponges down. They can wipe their fingers on the paper towels. Ask one student from each group (for instance, the blue tile student) to take all four tiles and quickly rinse them in the sink or rinse tub then bring them back to their group. Give students the challenge of deciding which tile they think got the cleanest and which they think stayed the dirtiest.

4. Let groups informally compare their tiles and share observations about which ingredients cleaned the best, while someone from each group takes the trays of ingredients and the sponges to a central location. They may want to put their tiles in order, from cleanest to least clean.

5. Ask someone from each table to report their group's findings to the class. Some groups may report ties between two ingredients for best cleaner. As in the previous session, record this information on the board under the heading "Cleaning Test," by putting a star for each group next to each ingredient chosen as best cleaner.

6. Encourage students to think about cause and effect by asking, "If you want your toothpaste to clean teeth well, which ingredient(s) would you be sure to put in?" Also ask, "If you put *only* soap in your toothpaste, what would your toothpaste be like?" [It would clean well and be foamy, but also slimy.] If no one mentions it, tell the class that another attribute of soap is that it does not taste good!

7. Have a student from each table collect the tiles and take them back to soak in the rinse tub.

Some students may have heard the negative phrase "go wash your mouth out with soap." If you feel that your class is not convinced that soap tastes bad, you may want to do the following optional demonstration: With the class watching, mix a bit of calcium carbonate with a few drops of water to make a paste; do the same thing with soap. Ask for a volunteer to come up and help with a taste test to decide which powder tastes the best for toothpaste making. Ask the volunteer to put her finger into the calcium carbonate paste and then to taste it. Ask her to describe the taste. Then do the same with the soap! Have a cup of water to sip or a small candy available to give the student to cover up the soap taste.

Note: Soap usually wins the cleaning test. Calcium carbonate's abrasiveness is also effective in scrubbing. Be prepared for the possibility that **results may vary in your class.** Differences in the blueberry stains or in how hard groups scrub are two of the possible reasons for this variation. That's okay—the goal of the activity is NOT to teach the idea of controlled experimentation—rather, the important focus is on **cause and effect** (if you put a certain ingredient in your toothpaste formula, your toothpaste will clean better).

Clean Up

1. Save trays with ingredient cups, spoons, popsicle sticks, and droppers for the next session. Stack them if you need to save space.

2. Save the color key of ingredients for Session 7.

3. Soak and rinse the sponges.

4. Soak tiles in a tub of water mixed with a tablespoon of bleach for a few hours or overnight. Give them a quick scrub and rinse. They can be re-used next time you do this unit.

5. Sponge off tables.

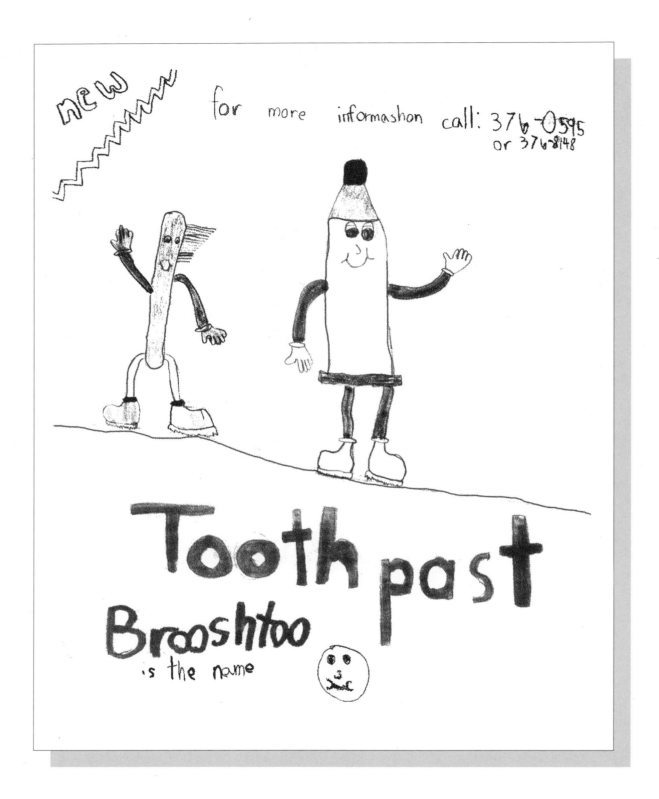

Session 7: Secret Formulas for Toothpaste

Overview

Using the information gathered during Sessions 5 and 6, your students now create their own secret formulas for toothpaste. They mix the ingredients in a ziplock bag, carefully recording each spoonful, drop, or scoop on a data sheet. To "cap" it all off, the young scientists get to take their bags of toothpaste home to brush their teeth.

Three additional flavor ingredients (vanilla and mint extracts, and lemon juice) are available in this session, adding several more exciting ingredient choices. As they add ingredients, students naturally become more aware of the effects of each. As they develop their own personal formulas, they constantly observe, measure, record and test, then adjust their ideas, make new predictions, and then test again with further mixing. As they refine the skills and concepts developed so far in this unit, your students are truly engaged in the practice of science!

What You Need

For the class:
- ❏ 16 oz. each: vanilla and mint extracts, and lemon juice
- ❏ 1 black permanent felt marker
- ❏ 1 large piece of white construction paper to extend the color key of ingredients begun in previous toothpaste sessions
- ❏ about 12 colored dots in two colors, preferably 6 yellow and 6 green (to label a few more cups)
- ❏ 1 pair of scissors
- ❏ 1 roll of plastic wrap
- ❏ 200 TUMS tablets *or* about 72 teaspoons (close to 2 cups) of powdered calcium carbonate
- ❏ 2 or more sponges

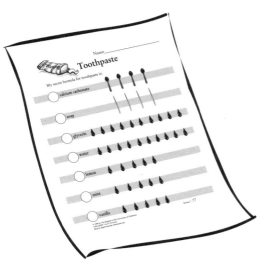

For each group of four students:
- ❏ 1 cafeteria tray
- ❏ orange, yellow, green, and blue-dot cups of ingredients with droppers, spoons, and popsicle sticks from previous toothpaste sessions
- ❏ 1 red-dot cup
- ❏ 2 new 8 to 10 oz. plastic cups
- ❏ 1 flat toothpick
- ❏ 3 more droppers
- ❏ students' personal cups
- ❏ 4 ziplock sandwich bags
- ❏ 4 Toothpaste data sheets (master on page 77)
- ❏ 4 pencils
- ❏ *(optional)* crayons in red, blue, yellow, green, and orange

If you haven't ground them already, you or an adult volunteer will need to crush or grind about 150–200 TUMS tablets for this session. (Please see "Getting Ready" in Session 5 for details.)

For information on ordering food grade calcium carbonate, please see the "Sources for Materials" section and read the information on calcium carbonate in "Behind the Scenes."

Getting Ready

Materials on Trays

1. **Replenish the cups.** If necessary, replenish the ingredient cups from earlier toothpaste sessions, and check to see that the droppers, spoons, and popsicle sticks are still in the cups. Remove the spoons and popsicle sticks from the soap cups. Put one toothpick in each soap cup. Have all four ingredient cups on a tray for each group.

Four ingredient cups from earlier toothpaste sessions:

- orange-dot cup: 2–3 tablespoons of calcium carbonate powder (ground TUMS)

- yellow dot-cup: about $1/8$ cup Ivory Snow soap (one ounce)

- green-dot cup: about $1/4$ cup glycerin (two ounces)

- blue-dot cup: about $1/4$ cup water (two ounces)

2. **Add new ingredient cups to trays.** Each group of students will need three more ingredient cups, for a total of seven. Fill the cups as follows:

Three ingredient cups added for this session:

- red-dot cup: about $1/4$ cup vanilla extract (two ounces)

- yellow **half**-dot cup: about $1/4$ cup lemon juice (two ounces)

- green **half**-dot cup: about $1/4$ cup mint extract (two ounces)

3. **Add droppers:** Put a dropper into each of the three new ingredient cups.

4. **Cover the extract cups.** To slow evaporation, put plastic wrap over the cups of extracts until just before the students will use them.

Materials Not on Trays

1. **Extend your class color key.** Add the extra ingredients (vanilla, lemon, mint) to your class color key, and stick the appropriate colored dot or half-dot next to each, so the color key now includes the following:

- orange-dot: calcium carbonate
- yellow-dot: soap
- green-dot: glycerin
- blue-dot: water
- red-dot: vanilla
- **half**-dot of yellow: lemon
- **half**-dot of green: mint

2. **Put initials on ziplock bags.** Using a permanent marker, write each student's initials on a ziplock bag. Have them ready to distribute at the beginning of the activity.

3. **Have personal cups handy.** Be ready to distribute these. They will be used to set the bags in, for stability.

4. **Prepare the data sheets.** Duplicate one Toothpaste data sheet per student (master on page 77), and decide if you will have students use crayons to color code the ingredients on the data sheet. Plan to have students color in half the dot for the last two ingredients.

GO!

Introducing the Activity

1. Ask if the ingredients they choose will make a difference in the attributes of their toothpaste. [yes!]

2. Take a minute to review the importance of consistency:

- Ask if anyone likes slimy or watery toothpaste. [No!!!] Why not? [It won't feel good in your mouth; won't stay on your toothbrush; won't scrub teeth well.]

- Ask, "Which ingredient(s) that we've used would you add if you wanted to make your toothpaste dryer and thicker?"

- Say that toothpaste shouldn't be too dry and thick, either, because it needs to be squeezed out of the tube and needs to spread around on your teeth. Ask, "Which ingredient(s) would you add if you wanted to make your toothpaste more squishy?"

3. Use your class color key to introduce the three new ingredients, saying that they are all flavorings.

- Tell students that if they don't know what these flavors taste like, they can get an idea if they might want to use them by smelling them first.

- Review how to waft the smells by using your hand to push the air above the cup toward your nose.

- Mention that they don't have to use all the flavors.

- Add that they'll only add a little of these strong flavors for taste or smell, so if they want to adjust the "feel" of their toothpaste, they should use water or glycerin instead.

Modeling How to Add and Mix Ingredients

1. Show students the bags they will use for mixing their own toothpastes. Their initials are on them, and yes, they may take them home!

2. Show how to set the bag into a personal cup so it won't tip over as easily while they measure and add ingredients.

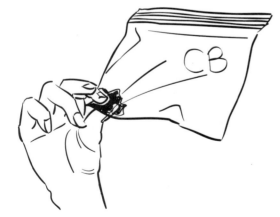

3. Model how to mix ingredients and also check how the mixture feels. Lift the bag out of the cup and hold it at an angle so the ingredients settle into one corner, and rub the mixture together through the bag.

4. Demonstrate how to measure a small scoop of soap using the flat end of the toothpick, and remind students how to measure drops (as opposed to dropperfuls or squirts) by holding the dropper vertically and squeezing gently.

Modeling How to Record on the Data Sheet

1. Pass out data sheets and have students color code the names of the ingredients (if you have decided this is desirable).

2. Show how to record how much of each ingredient they add. Each time they put in a spoonful of calcium carbonate, they circle a spoon on the sheet. For soap, they circle a toothpick, and for the rest, they circle a drop each time they add one. Stress that careful scientific record-keeping prevents having a secret formula that is a secret from the inventor too!

3. Explain that there are some **limits** to the amounts of the ingredients that can be used. Ask the students to look at the data sheet and tell you, "What is the MOST calcium carbonate a person can use?" [four spoons] Explain that for the other ingredients, they can use as much or as many as they want, up to a limit of whatever amount is shown on the sheet. (No more than ten drops of glycerin, six drops of lemon, etc.)

Let the Toothpaste Making Begin!

1. Have someone pass out the labeled ziplock bags and personal cups. Have one student from each group get a tray, and let the students begin.

2. Check that students are recording each spoonful, scoop, or drop **as they add it.** As students show you their toothpastes in progress, you may want to ask what else they could add to make it more like commercial toothpaste (often student toothpaste starts out dry or gluey).

3. As groups finish, have them put all the materials except their bags of toothpaste back on the trays. Have one student from each group take the trays to a central location, and have students sponge off their tables.

4. Have students seal their bags. Ask how they might test this toothpaste to see if it is good. [brush at home] Ask the class if toothpaste is food [NO!] Remind them that although they know it is not to be eaten, they should keep it away from younger siblings.

Surprisingly, many students are satisfied with a final product that you might not find acceptable yourself!

Going Further

1. Encourage students to create a magazine advertisement for their toothpaste, calling attention to its attributes.

2. Research the actual ingredients in several commercial toothpastes (see "Behind the Scenes").

3. The class could make a graph showing their favorite toothpastes. Have students brainstorm a list of different brands of toothpaste they have used. Create a graph of their personal favorites. What criteria did they use to choose their favorite brands? Students can survey their family members and create another graph of their families' preferences. Compare the two graphs. What are the similarities? Differences? Who might be interested in analyzing this data?

4. Shopping for Toothpaste: Have students find out the prices of the three favorite brands of toothpaste at local stores. Record the prices for the brands at different stores. Be sure to agree on the size of the tube or container that the toothpastes come in to make the comparisons fair. What is the range in cost for each brand of toothpaste? Why would there be a range? What is the difference in price from the most inexpensive to the most expensive toothpaste? What is the cost of one ounce of each toothpaste? Why would one toothpaste cost more money than another brand? What is the actual cost of the ingredients that go into toothpaste?

Calculators can be a very useful tool in figuring out these costs. This provides a great opportunity to use calculators in context to help young students solve problems that would otherwise be too challenging.

The Feel Test

The Foam Test

Preventing decay

Cleaning and polishing

Brush germs away

Taste is important

Healthy teeth too

What's the best toothpaste —

Designed by you!

Toothpaste

My secret formula for toothpaste is:

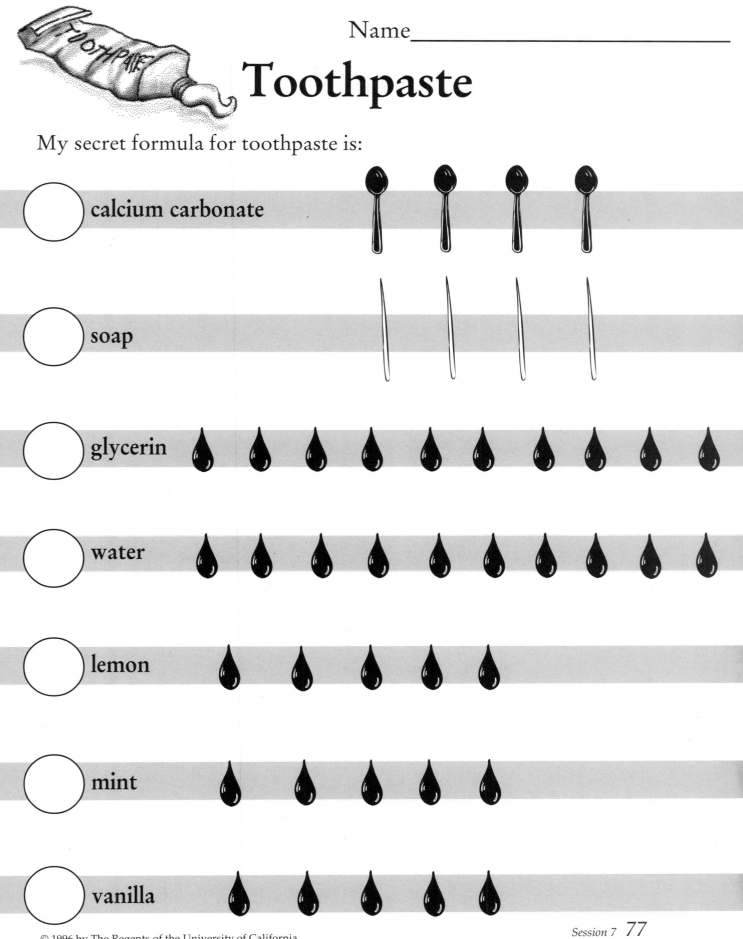

calcium carbonate

soap

glycerin

water

lemon

mint

vanilla

Session 8: Ice Cream Testing

Overview

You begin this session by introducing the ingredients of ice cream—modeling how to measure, mix, and record them. Although students won't use the milk, sugar, flavoring, and color until Session 9, you model for them now how they will mix them in a cup and then place them in a ziplock bag. Holding up your bag of ingredients, you ask, "Is this ice cream?" No! It needs to be **cold!**

Putting aside your bag of ice cream ingredients, you focus the class for the rest of this session on the question of temperature. Groups of students use their fingers to test the temperature difference between cups of plain ice and ice to which they've added rock salt. The rock salt and ice mixture is noticeably colder. Next, they put bags of water into the cups to see if they freeze.

During the ten minutes or so they need to wait, you read the students a story related to cold and freezing or to the entire *Secret Formulas* unit. When they return to their experiment, the students are amazed and excited to find that the water bags in the rock salt and ice mixture have frozen (yes, it really works!), but the ones in the plain ice have not.

You may have your own favorite books. See the "Literature Connections" section for suggestions.

By the end of this session, the concept of cause and effect will have further "solidified"—rock salt causes ice to get colder. The students will realize that rock salt will be important to use when freezing their own special ice creams.

Special Note: As with the cola activity, be sensitive to dietary restrictions that some students may have. In the ice cream activities, milk allergies may be a concern. Other liquids, such as mocha mix or other soy- or rice-based beverages can be substituted. You may also need to take special measures regarding sugar for some students.

What You Need

For the class:
- ❏ 1 bag of ice cubes or crushed ice, about 5 lbs.
- ❏ access to a nearby freezer or a cooler to store ice
- ❏ 3 lbs. rock salt (about 4 cups)
- ❏ 1 black permanent felt marker
- ❏ 1 ziplock sandwich bag
- ❏ your own personal cup from earlier sessions
- ❏ 3 color-coded plastic cups (one each: blue dot, green dot, orange dot)
- ❏ 3 oz. regular milk
- ❏ $1/2$ cup white sugar
- ❏ $1/8$ cup vanilla extract (about 1 oz.)
- ❏ $1/8$ cup strawberry extract (about 1 oz.)
- ❏ 1 roll of plastic wrap
- ❏ 1 small, lightweight plastic spoon
- ❏ 1 popsicle stick
- ❏ 1 plastic stirrer
- ❏ 2 droppers
- ❏ 3 squeeze bottles of food coloring (red, yellow, blue)
- ❏ 1 piece of 8 $1/2$" x 11" white construction paper
- ❏ 3 dots (blue, green, orange) for the color key
- ❏ 1 dump bucket or access to a sink
- ❏ 1 piece of butcher paper or chalkboard

For each group of four students:
- ❏ 1 cafeteria tray
- ❏ 3 plastic cups (1 red dot, 1 yellow dot, 1 green half-dot)
- ❏ 1 small, lightweight plastic spoon
- ❏ 1 popsicle stick
- ❏ 2 ziplock sandwich bags

Getting Ready

Getting Ready for your Ice Cream Ingredients Demonstration

1. **Make a color key.** Write the three ingredients below on a large sheet of paper and put the appropriately colored dots near each. Have the color key handy near where you will introduce the activity.

- blue: sugar
- green: vanilla
- orange: strawberry

2. **Draw an enlarged version of the data sheet on the chalkboard.** List the ingredients and draw the same number of spoons and drops that are on the Ice Cream data sheet (page 97). This should be on the chalkboard near where you will introduce the activity. You will use this to model how to record your demonstration secret formula. (The students will use their sheets in the next session.)

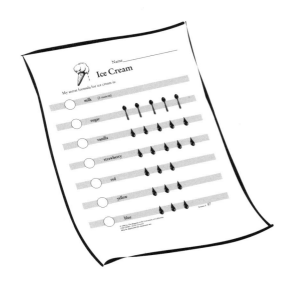

3. **Fill four plastic cups with ingredients for your demonstration.** (*You don't prepare ingredient cups for student groups until the next session.*)

- blue: Fill with about half a cup of sugar. Put a spoon and a popsicle stick in the sugar cup.

- green: $^1/_4$ cup (2 ounces) vanilla extract and a dropper (cover with plastic wrap).

- orange: $^1/_4$ cup (2 ounces) strawberry extract and a dropper (cover with plastic wrap).

- your personal cup: Pour milk up to the bottom of your initials (3 ounces). Put a plastic stirrer in the cup.

Some teachers prefer to make an overhead transparency of the student data sheet.

4. **Set up your demonstration materials for ice cream ingredients.** (You don't need the rock salt or ice for this demonstration.)

- The blue, green, and orange cups of ingredients
- Your personal cup with three ounces of milk and stirrer
- An empty ziplock bag with your initials on it
- The three squeeze bottles of food coloring (red, yellow, blue)

Getting Ready for the Ice and Rock Salt Activity

1. **Prepare ziplock bags.** Each group of four will need two ziplock sandwich bags. Fill each bag with about a tablespoon of water, and seal it. (The water does not need to be measured accurately.) Have the bags handy and ready to distribute.

2. **Choose a storybook to read during the session.** During the latter part of the session, while students are waiting for results in the ice experiment, you'll need to gather them away from their materials for a story of about 10 minutes. Decide now where you will gather the students for the story. If possible, try to choose a story related to freezing or ice cream or to the entire *Secret Formulas* unit. (See the "Literature Connections" section for some suggested storybooks.)

3. **Set up trays of materials.** Assemble the following materials on a tray for each group of four students. Wait until just before starting the activity to put the ice in the cups.

- red-dot cup: Fill half full with rock salt, and add one spoon and popsicle stick.

- yellow-dot cup: Fill half full of ice.

- green **half**-dot cup: Fill half full of ice.

Add ice just before distributing to students

Introducing Ice Cream Ingredients

1. Tell students that in the next class session, they will be making secret formulas for ice cream! Discuss homemade ice cream and ways students may have made it. Ask them to think about and describe the attributes of ice cream, and list their responses on the chalkboard. Prompt them by asking what they like about ice cream. [it is sweet, cold, minty (or whatever flavor), smooth]

2. Point out the Ice Cream data sheet you've drawn on the chalkboard, and give students a preview of the seven ingredients they'll get to choose from when creating their own ice cream.

3. Emphasize that there are only two **flavors** (vanilla and strawberry). Explain that the red, blue, and yellow colors are just **coloring,** and won't add flavor to the ice cream.

4. Show your cup with milk up to the initials. Say that everyone will get the same amount of milk, but they'll choose how much of the other ingredients they want to use for their secret formulas.

Modeling How to Add Ingredients

1. Ask students to refer to the number of drops or spoons on your chalkboard data sheet, and tell you the **most** you can use (five spoons sugar, four drops vanilla, etc.).

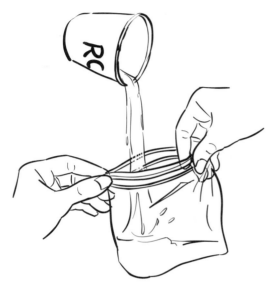

2. Add your choice of ingredients to the cup of milk—for instance, three level spoons of sugar, four drops of vanilla flavor, and one drop of yellow food coloring. Model how to record amounts by circling the appropriate number of spoons or drops on the chalkboard data sheet.

3. Ask a volunteer to help you by holding open a ziplock bag. Pour the ice cream ingredients from your personal cup into the bag. Hold up the bag and ask, "Is this ice cream?" [No! It isn't cold or hard.]

4. Ask how to make the ice cream cold. Many students will say to add ice. Clarify that the ice isn't an ingredient—it doesn't go *in* the ice cream. It goes near it to make it cold.

Introducing Rock Salt and Ice

1. Put your bag of ice cream ingredients aside, and use one of the trays of ice and rock salt to introduce the next activity.

2. Tell the students that, to get ready for making ice cream next time, they are going to learn more about ice today. Say that lots of people mix rock salt with ice when they make ice cream. Hold up the cup of rock salt, and say it's a kind of salt that comes in big chunks. **Emphasize that they are not to taste it.**

3. Say that you'd like them to test what happens when they add rock salt to ice. Show the two cups of ice, one with a yellow dot, and the other with a green half-dot.

Ice with 4 spoonfuls of rock salt

Ice with no rock salt

4. Tell them they will add four level spoonfuls of rock salt to the yellow-dot cup, and leave the green half-dot cup with just ice in it. Remind them how to level the spoonfuls with the popsicle stick. (To encourage full participation, you might want to suggest that each person in the group add one spoonful of salt to the yellow-dot cup.)

5. Say that they will all get to put their fingers in the cups of ice to feel which one is colder. Tell them that they should share the cups so everyone can reach both of them. They should gently wiggle their fingers around near the bottom of the cups. They may need to try a few times to be sure. (The difference probably won't be noticeable until a few minutes after they put in the salt.)

6. Say that if their fingers get too cold, they should pull them out for a while. You might also want to mention that since their fingers might get salty, they should not rub their eyes, because that might sting a little.

7. Quickly add ice to the cups on trays. Distribute the trays, and have groups begin. When all students have had enough time to feel the cups of ice for at least a minute or so, have everyone remove their fingers from the cups.

8. Regain the attention of the class, and ask the students what they felt. Have them vote on which cup they thought was colder. Ask which they think would be better for making ice cream cold, plain ice or ice and rock salt. (If some students are not sure, that is all right. The next test will be more conclusive.)

A Freezing Test

1. Hold up one of the ziplock bags of water you prepared earlier, and tilt it so the water collects in one corner of the bag. Explain that each group will get two of these bags of water. Tell them that they are going to see what happens when they put the bags into their two cups.

2. Show the students how to bury the water-filled corner of the bag in an ice cup. Suggest that they make a little "hole" in their ice, put the corner of the bag into the hole, and then cover that part of the bag with ice.

3. Ask for predictions about what might happen to the water in the bags. [It might freeze.] Tell them that once they have buried both bags, they should go to the group area for a story. Explain that it takes time for things to freeze so they are going to let the ice cups sit while they listen to a story.

The goal of this activity is to reinforce the concept of cause and effect. It is not important that primary students learn the chemistry of why rock salt makes ice colder. However, if you would like more information about this, please see the "Behind the Scenes" section.

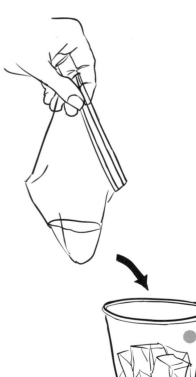

4. Distribute two bags to each group. As groups finish burying their bags, have them come to the area where you will read the story.

5. Read the story for at least 10 minutes. (Up to 20 minutes is fine.)

Checking the Results of the Freezing Test

1. While still away from the materials, remind the class that the goal is to find out how they can best make their ice cream cold. By looking at what happened to the water, they may find out something.

2. Tell them that when they get to their tables, they should take their bags out of both cups, and let everyone in the group see what happened to them.

3. Have them go to check their bags. After a few minutes, have them leave their materials and return to the area where you read the story.

4. Ask for their observations. Ask what they should use when they want to freeze their personal bag of ice cream ingredients. [ice and rock salt]

Clean Up

1. Have students dump all of the ice into the sink or a dump bucket.

2. Rinse the ice cups and set them out to air dry. If you would like to save and re-use the ziplock bags, rinse any salt off the outsides, empty them of water and turn them inside out to dry. Save the cups of rock salt with spoons and popsicle sticks for the next session.

3. Save the set of cups of ingredients you used in your demonstration. If you have a refrigerator handy, your demonstration ice cream bag can also be saved to be frozen in the next session.

Going Further

1. You might want to ask the students how they could freeze the water in the bag that was in just the ice. [They could add rock salt to the ice or could move the bags to the other cup which contains the mixture of salt and ice]. Have the students try out their ideas, or try their ideas as a demonstration which the students can check back on later, to see what happened.

2. With older students, this session can provide a great opportunity to look at temperature in more detail. Students could, for example, measure and record the temperature of both the ice and the ice with rock salt. They could also measure the temperature of the water in different buckets around the classroom. It's also fun to let them stick their fingers in while they measure, so they gain experience with how different temperatures feel. Should your classrooms be fortunate enough to have access to a temperature probe that can be used with a personal computer, you could generate revealing graphs and do very interesting studies of the temperature changes.

Rock salt with ice
Does something quite nice
Try it and see
We're sure you'll agree
No foolin'
It's coolin'!

From this who would dream—
We'd discover ice cream!

Session 9: Secret Formulas for Ice Cream

Overview

In this scrumptious session, each student mixes ice cream ingredients in a cup, then pours them into a ziplock sandwich bag, following the procedure you modeled in the previous session, to create their very own ice cream. Students can now bring to bear all the experience they've gained throughout the unit, to help them with the delicate and delicious processes of measuring, mixing, recording, evaluating, and adjusting.

Each group of students adds rock salt to a freezer bag of ice, and all four students put their bags of ice cream ingredients into the freezer bag. Then they put their freezer bag into a T-shirt, grasp the ends of the T-shirt and shake! When their ice cream is frozen, they open the bags and enjoy.

After their ice cream is only a very happy memory, each student still possesses a carefully-recorded personal secret formula that they can use at home to re-create the same exact refreshing snack. But they also come away from this session and the entire unit with something even more valuable than that: a strong grasp of key scientific and mathematical skills, concepts, and processes; a variety of experiences that build toward more sophisticated understandings of experimentation and invention; and an overwhelmingly positive (and tasty) experience with "doing science."

One teacher told us, "They were very excited about eating ice cream, so they were very careful about following directions and not spilling any of their ingredients." Another said, "I saw their measuring skills improve greatly as compared to when they started out in Session 1."

What You Need

For the class:
- ❏ access to a nearby freezer or cooler
- ❏ 1 gallon regular milk (allow about a quart per 10 students, plus a quart extra)
- ❏ 3 lbs. of white sugar (about 6 cups)
- ❏ 3 5-lb. bags of crushed ice (or ice cubes)
- ❏ 3 lbs. rock salt (about 4 cups)
- ❏ 6 small squeeze bottles of food coloring (two bottles each: red, blue, yellow)
- ❏ students' personal cups
- ❏ 16 oz. vanilla extract
- ❏ 16 oz. strawberry extract
- ❏ 1 roll or stack of paper towels
- ❏ 32 clean plastic spoons (for eating ice cream)
- ❏ a dozen extra ziplock sandwich bags
- ❏ a few extra ziplock gallon-size freezer bags
- ❏ 2 rinse buckets
- ❏ 1 black permanent felt marker
- ❏ stack of newspapers for spills
- ❏ sponges
- ❏ (optional) mop and bucket

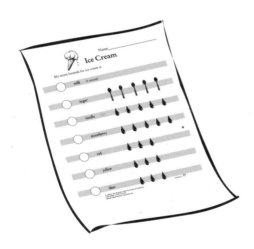

For each group of four students:
- ❏ 1 cafeteria tray
- ❏ 3 color-coded plastic cups (blue, green, orange)
- ❏ 2 small, lightweight plastic spoons
- ❏ 2 droppers
- ❏ 2 popsicle sticks
- ❏ 4 plastic stirrers
- ❏ 1 red-dot cup with rock salt from Session 8
- ❏ 1 gallon-size ziplock *freezer* bag*
- ❏ 4 ziplock sandwich bags
- ❏ 1 T-shirt (adult-sized)
- ❏ 4 Ice Cream data sheets (master on page 97)
- ❏ pencils
- ❏ (optional) crayons or markers in blue, green, and orange

*We recommend using the more expensive, sturdier freezer bags, because regular gallon-size ziplock bags sometimes leak. It is also possible to rinse and re-use these stronger freezer bags. We know that the Glad brand of these freezer bags works well.

Getting Ready

Before the Day of the Activity

1. Decide where the students will shake their ice cream.
During the first part of the session, students will work in
their groups of four at tables, to mix ingredients. Later
they need to stand up and shake their ice cream. (Every
group will put their four individual ice cream bags into a
large freezer bag of ice and rock salt, and put that into a T-
shirt "sling" for shaking!) Not only is this bound to be a
noisy activity, but the bags often drip salty water.
Needless to say, the **shaking should be done outdoors if
at all possible!** If you must stay indoors, have a mop and
bucket available.

2. Arrange for adult volunteers. We strongly recommend
that you arrange to have two or more adult volunteers in
your classroom during this session. Plan for help during
set-up and clean up too, if possible. It's nice to have two
adults to distribute the drops of food coloring to the
students and to check the seals on their bags before they
shake. Extra adult supervision and more helpful hands
will make the shaking activity easier for all.

3. Arrange for some extra ice cream to be made. Ask one
of the volunteers to mix a few extra ziplock bags of ice
cream ingredients during the activity. (Some groups of
students can shake an extra bag along with theirs in the T-
shirt.) This way, there will be extra ice cream to eat for
students who accidentally get salt from the outside of their
bags in their ice cream. See information about removing
salt on page 95.

On the Day of the Activity

Materials on Trays

1. Prepare ingredient cups. Fill three color-coded plastic
cups for each group of students, and put them on a tray.

- blue-dot cup: about $3/4$ cup of sugar
- green-dot cup: about $1/4$ cup vanilla extract (two
  ounces)
- orange-dot cup: about $1/4$ cup strawberry extract
  (two ounces)

2. **Add droppers, popsicle sticks, and spoons.** Put two small plastic spoons and two popsicle sticks in each blue-dot cup. Put a dropper into each cup of extract.

3. **Add four stirrers to each tray.** Each student will need a stirrer to mix their ingredients in their personal cup before pouring them into the ziplock bag.

Materials Not on Trays

1. **Post the color key.** Have the color key for ingredients from Session 8 on the wall where students can see it.

2. **Prepare student data sheets.** Make a copy of the Ice Cream data sheet for each student (master on page 97).

3. **Replenish the red-dot cups from the previous session with rock salt.** Fill each cup half full, and remove the spoon and stirrer. There should be one red-dot cup per group of four students. Each group will pour the entire half-cup of rock salt into their bag of ice. Have the red-dot cups near the ice bags, so that students can easily add the rock salt when they are ready to shake their ice cream. (The rock salt should not be on the group's tray of materials, because of the complication that someone might think it's an ingredient for the ice cream!)

4. **Fill the ice bags.** For each group of students, fill one ziplock freezer bag about half full of ice. If possible, keep the ice in a cooler or freezer until just before it is needed.

5. **Put initials on small bags.** Use a permanent marker to write each student's initials on a ziplock sandwich bag. Have them ready to distribute at the beginning of the activity.

6. **Have personal cups ready.** Have personal cups clean and ready to pass out.

7. **Have milk ready to pour into personal cups.** Keep the milk in a cooler until it's time to pour.

8. **Prepare rinse bucket(s) and waste container.** Fill a rinse bucket (or two) half full with cold tap water, and put it in the area where students will do the ice cream shaking. Have an empty bucket or dishpan to use as a container for ice bags, T-shirts, and other materials at the end of the shaking activity.

9. **Have food coloring ready for adults to distribute.** Decide whether adult volunteers will come to student groups, or whether they will sit at a "color station" and students will go to them when they are ready for drops of coloring.

10. **Have plastic spoons handy.** Have clean plastic spoons ready for distribution at the end of the activity.

Reviewing Ingredients and Amounts

1. *(Optional)* Pass out Ice Cream data sheets, and have students color code the ingredients according to the color key. Remind students that first they'll mix milk and other ingredients in their cups, then add the mixture to a ziplock bag.

2. **Adding milk.** Say that everyone will add the same amount of milk. Tell the students that you or another adult will pour milk into their personal cups up to the bottom of their initials.

3. **Adding sugar.** Say that after they add each spoonful, they can stir with a stirrer, and taste a little bit of the mixture to see if it is sweet enough. Remind them that ice cream is like cola; the more sugar they add, the sweeter it will be. Re-emphasize the five spoonful limit for sugar. Remind the students to circle the number of spoons of sugar they use on their Ice Cream data sheet.

4. **Adding flavor.** Review the two flavor choices. [vanilla and strawberry] Ask, "What's the most vanilla and strawberry you can add?" [ten—five drops of each] Urge the students to smell the flavors before adding them. Tell them that it is a good idea to taste their mixture after adding each drop. Remind them that they cannot take out an ingredient once it's in and to record the flavor on their data sheet.

5. **Adding color.** Review the color choices. [red, yellow, blue] Ask, "Are these colors also flavors?" [no, just colors] Explain that your adult helpers will add these drops for them. They will need to decide which color(s) and how many drops. In this case, they are limited to a total of not more than three drops. For example, they could pick one drop of each color, or two red drops and one yellow, etc. They'll record their selections on their data sheets so the helpers can follow their recipe.

6. **Pouring the mixture into the bag.** Explain that, working with a partner, they will pour their mixture of ingredients into the bag with their initials on it. Demonstrate having a partner hold the bag until the mixture is poured, and the bag zipped up. Caution the students to be careful that their bag is sealed well before setting it down.

Explaining the Ice and Shaking Procedures

1. Explain that after they have poured their mixtures into their bags, all four of these bags will go into one big ice bag for their group. This means they must wait for their complete group of four to be ready before the ice cream can be shaken. **Again, tell them to be sure their own personal ice cream bag is sealed well.** (You may want to demonstrate sealing the bag and making sure all the air is out by placing the bag on a table, pressing to push the air out and sealing it, at first in an upright position, and then over the edge of the table. This will help ensure the bags do not pop open.)

2. Say that when their group goes to get their ice bag, they will also get one red-dot cup of rock salt to pour into their bag. (There is no need to layer the salt and ice, as in traditional ice cream makers.) Then they will put their group's four small bags of ice cream ingredients into the ice bag. Say that they should zip the ice bag up very carefully.

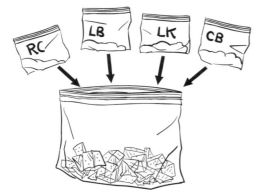

Team places individual ice cream bags into a large ziplock freezer bag containing ice and rock salt

3. Show the groups how to put the bag into the T-shirt. Have one student hold one end of the shirt closed and one student hold the other end, then tell them to start shaking the bags back and forth or up and down. Mention that the shaking does not need to be fast. Bags need to be shaken continuously for about five minutes.

4. Groups should share the shaking job. Two students could shake for a few minutes and then give their partners a turn. Some groups may find a way for all four students to shake at once. After a few minutes, they can check to see if their ice cream is getting frozen. If not, they need to keep shaking!

Let the Ice Cream Making Begin!

1. When you finish your introduction, and while students are thinking about which ingredients and amounts they will use, have a student from each group come and get a tray of ingredients.

2. Have several helpers pass out the personal cups and bags, and have an adult fill each student's personal cup with milk, up to the bottom of their initials (approximately three ounces).

3. Circulate, making sure that students are recording their ingredients as they add them. As students finish adding the other ingredients, have an adult or two add food coloring, and help with sealing the bags.

4. Let the groups get ice bags, rock salt, and T-shirts, and begin shaking. Supervise the shaking, making sure everyone in a group gets a chance to participate.

5. As they finish, have students dip their small bags into the rinse tub and rinse them. After they rinse off the salt, the outside of their bag may still be a bit salty. Help students fold the top of their bag outward so that they will be less likely to get salt in their ice cream. **IMPORTANT: Take all measures to ensure that salt does not get into ice cream. Using fingers and water, clean away all salt that may have settled near the seal. Have a few extra bags of ice cream made in case some students need it.**

6. Hand out the spoons and watch them enjoy. Circulate and ask students how they think their secret formula for their very own special brand of ice cream came out.

7. Collect bags, spoons, and clean up.

*If you have decided that they will do the shaking outside, have an adult volunteer stationed outside with the big ice bags and the T-shirts. This allows for a smooth transition and provides extra supervision. Have the rinse bucket and spoons outside too, so when their ice cream shaking is done, students can rinse the salt off their bags and enjoy an outdoor ice cream event. **It's a good idea to clean any salt off the outer part of the seal with water and fingers, before opening the bags.** Also set out the empty bucket to put used ice bags and T-shirts in, and a place to discard their ice cream bags when they're done eating.*

Going Further

1. Ask students to write or draw the story of how they made their ice cream. You may want to suggest that they do this in a step-by-step cartoon fashion, describing the main steps in the process, and then write a paragraph on how their ice cream tasted.

2. Have students create an advertisement for their special ice cream, highlighting its attributes.

3. Ask students to write another formula with all the ingredients they could possibly want in an ice cream (creamier milk, fresh strawberries, chocolate, marshmallows, nuts, etc.).

4. Students could do an all-school survey or make a class graph of favorite ice cream flavors.

5. You can also use ice cream cones for a fun mathematics activity. Pretend you are in an ice cream shop that sells cones with two scoops of ice cream on each cone. If the flavors that they have are chocolate, vanilla, and strawberry, how many different two-scoop cones could you create with those three flavors? (*Note:* This is a very open-ended problem! Have students draw out their solutions to explain their thinking! No one said there can't be two scoops of the same flavor, so some students may include chocolate/chocolate, vanilla/vanilla and strawberry/strawberry as possible answers! Other students may say that a chocolate scoop on the bottom and a vanilla scoop on top is different from a vanilla scoop on the bottom and chocolate on top!) After students do this problem, increase the flavors of ice cream to four, then five, and even six flavors. You may want to challenge older students with 3-scoop cones! Happy scooping!

6. Discuss the importance of scientific testing to product development. Talk about the process scientists may have gone through to find the right formula for shampoo, M&M's, or another product. Ask students what attributes scientists would look for in one of these products and what tests they might have to do. Challenge students to choose a favorite product and draw a picture showing how scientists might test for the attributes of this product.

Name_____

Ice Cream

My secret formula for ice cream is:

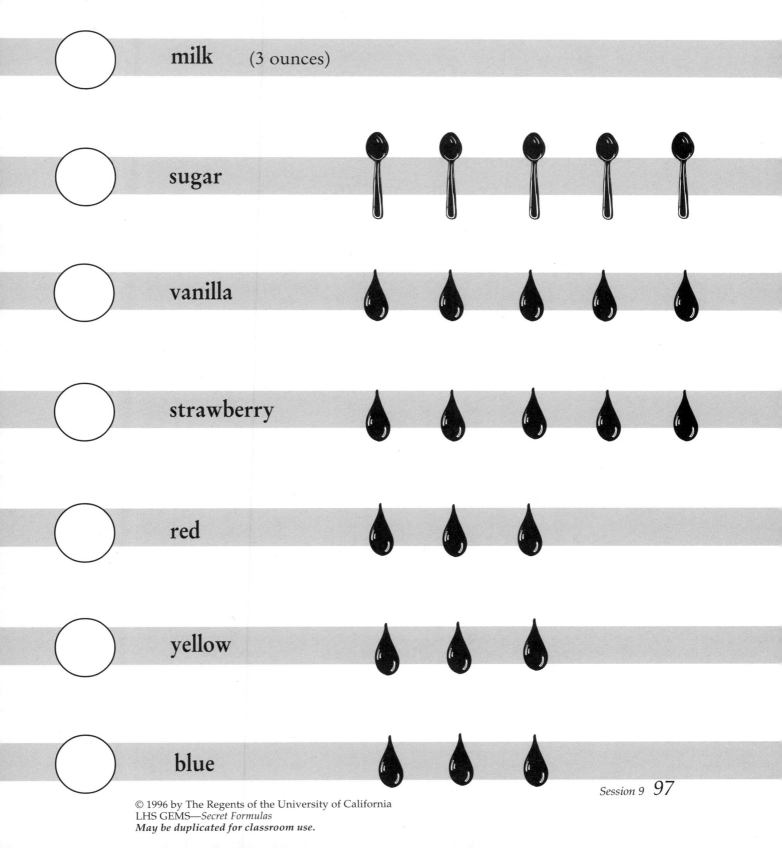

( ) **milk** (3 ounces)

( ) sugar

( ) vanilla

( ) strawberry

( ) red

( ) yellow

( ) blue

Going Further (for the entire unit)

1. **Paste Revisited.** Challenge students to use their new knowledge regarding secret formulas and recording data as they revisit the paste-making activity. Ask students to make paste again, only this time they will record their formula. Ask students to record their formulas on a blank piece of paper and instruct them to add sentences describing their thinking behind the ingredient choices and amounts.

2. **Inventions by Mistake.** Ask students to work as a class or in groups to research the history of unplanned inventions. See the "Behind the Scenes" and "Resources" sections in this guide for some ideas. Students may choose to study the story of post-its, velcro, or liquid soap. Encourage students to present the information to the rest of the class orally, in a letter, or through a dramatization.

3. **Other Products.** There are a number of other products of a household nature whose ingredients lend themselves, or can be adapted, to similar classroom activities. These can in turn continue to help your students strengthen their understanding of cause and effect, connect to many real-life items, and build student confidence in their own powers of invention. These include breakfast cereal, hand lotion, potting soil, and many more.

4. **Consumer Science.** Activities for this same age range that involve students in consumer science, comparing different brands of common items, etc. would also make good "going furthers" for this unit. The GEMS guide, *Paper Towel Testing*, for example, could be adapted for younger students.

5. **Product Scientists.** Consider inviting a scientist or research professional who works in the field of product testing to the class to describe how they use scientific tests to develop safe and useful products.

Please send us your suggestions for other extension ideas!

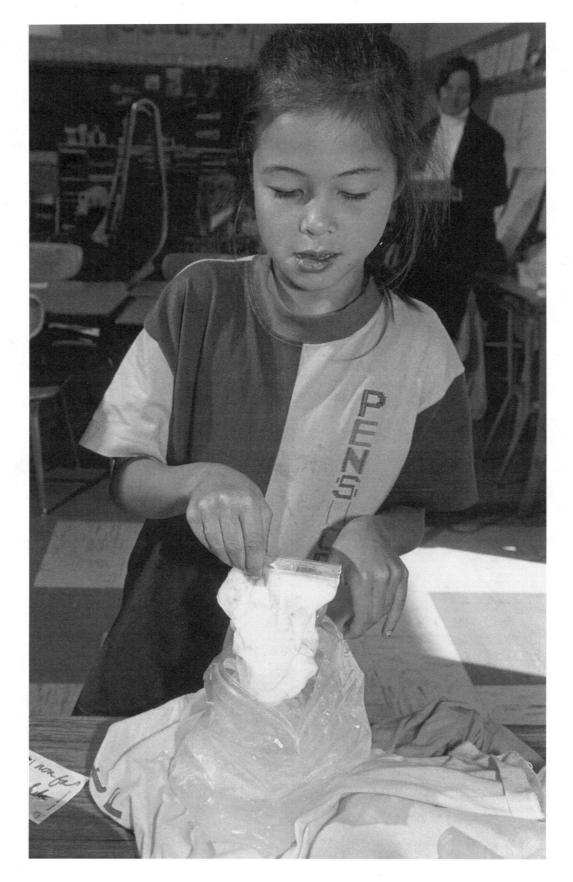

Behind the Scenes

The following information is designed to provide you, the teacher, with some basic background information for these activities, in response to questions your students may ask. It is organized by product, as is the teacher's guide: Paste, Cola, Toothpaste, and Ice Cream. This information is **not** meant to be read out loud to or copied for students. Additional information on each of the products can be found in the "Resources" section following this background section. Because these activities encourage the creative inventiveness of your students, we've also added a background section called "Mistakes that Worked" to provide a few examples of how some famous products were invented. We also list several related books in the "Resources" section.

Paste

What makes paste paste?

Adhesives are substances that hold materials together by surface attachment. All adhesives come in very close contact with the surface of the material, or substrate, with which they form a bond.

In order for an adhesive bond to form, the molecules of the adhesive must physically penetrate, actually hook into, the surface molecules of the substrate. This is why many adhesives start out wet, to better attach to the surface and then harden into a strong film that holds the surfaces together. Most of the adhesives used on paper have a water base. Paper is a porous substrate that allows for the evaporation of water. The bond forms during the process of evaporation.

Most pastes are made up of polymers, which are long chains of repeating groups of atoms. When the adhesive is wet, the polymers actually hook into the surface of the substrate. As the adhesive dries and sets, the molecules of the adhesive cross-link into each other, forming a film that sticks to itself.

The main ingredients of paste are starch and water. Starch found in wheat, rice, corn, and tubers is a good adhesive and it is a natural polymer. Starch molecules are long chains of sugar molecules linked together.

Three "true glues" (those which do not contain chemicals, compounds, or high technology substances) are hide (sometimes called skin) glue, bone glue, and fish glue. All are actually impure forms of gelatin made from the protein in the connective tissue of animals. When the animal tissues are heated in water a clear solution is produced which cools into gelatin. After it dries, the gelatin can be dissolved in water to form a liquid glue. This is the white or casein glue so commonly used (such as Elmer's glue).

Brief History of Paste

Native peoples from every area in the world have used glues to make things for thousands of years. Animal glues came into being when ancient tribes found they could process hides, skins, bones, and sinew into sticky substances. Early humans discovered that they could make a fish glue from the inner skins of the swim bladders of fish. Vegetable glues were prepared by ancient peoples from various plant matter—most parts of the world have some flora that seems to be sticky by nature.

Furniture found in the tombs of ancient Egyptian rulers, dating back 35 centuries, displays examples of fine veneers and ivory inlays glued to wooden bases. Other early civilizations, such as the Assyrians, Babylonians, Greeks, and Romans used glues made from many sources, such as blood, bones, hide, vegetables, grains, eggs, and milk. Famous cabinetmakers such as Sheraton and Chippendale also used glue made from bones and hides. Glues were used to attach feathers to arrows and, in more modern times, to fasten World War I propellers on fighting planes. Casein glue made from milk was used for this latter purpose due to its strength and resistance to moisture. With breakthroughs in chemistry and the plastics industry, many new "glues" have been created, including the powerfully bonding "super" glues of diverse kinds that have become part of modern life.

Coca-Cola

What makes Coca-Cola?

Now that's a billion dollar question! Although the exact formula for Coca-Cola remains a secret, we do know the basic ingredients of Coca-Cola. It is mostly made of carbonated water and sweetener. In addition caramel, phosphoric acid, natural flavors, and caffeine are listed as ingredients.

According to information supplied by the Coca-Cola Company, the amount of sugar in cola is comparable to that in fruit juice. An 8-ounce glass of Coca-Cola contains 27 grams of sugar (97 calories), compared to apple juice, which has 28 grams of sugar per 8-ounce serving (111 calories). Coca-Cola also cites the Food and Drug Administration in saying that sugar is safe, except for its link to tooth decay, and that there is no substantive evidence to prove a cause-and-effect relationship between sugar consumption and hyperactivity.

Ingredient information on the Coca-Cola bottle lists the sweetener as corn syrup, which is a thick, sweet syrup with a smooth texture. The syrup is made by mixing cornstarch with water, and adding an enzyme molecule in a process that converts the starch into two sugars, glucose and maltose. If an even sweeter syrup is desired, another enzyme is added which converts the sugar to fructose.

The natural flavors used in Coca-Cola are a secret, but some say the flavors include the ingredients vanilla, citric acid, and lime juice. One source, who claims to have seen the original recipe, says that an additional mixture was added, consiting of orange oil, lemon oil, nutmeg oil, cinnamon oil, coriander oil, neroli oil, and alcohol.

Coca-Cola Classic has 31 milligrams of caffeine per 8-ounce serving. This is one-fourth the caffeine in coffee and half the caffeine in tea.

Brief History of Coca-Cola

John Styth ("Doc") Pemberton was a retired Confederate cavalry colonel who worked as a pharmacist in Atlanta during the late 1800s. Pharmacists at that time brewed many home remedies designed to cure ills and benefit health. In 1886, Doc Pemberton boiled a new version of his French Wine of Coca, this time removing the wine. Hoping to obtain some of the new soda-fountain market, he used extract of the kola nut and coca leaves. These ingredients had a stimulating effect (they are commonly known as caffeine and cocaine). He then added quite a bit of sugar and a blend of flavors such as caramel, lime juice, nutmeg, cinnamon, and vanilla. At a nearby drugstore, they added carbonated soda water—this produced the first version of Coca-Cola.

The drink was first advertised as a medicinal product and, despite its addictive ingredients, reportedly had sluggish sales. In 1891, the product rights were sold to Griggs Candler who ordered that the recipe be kept a secret and targeted advertising toward the soft drink market. He gave away millions of clocks, bottle openers, bookmarks, pencils, and rulers with the trademark "Coca-Cola" printed on them. By the early 1900s, the use of cocaine in Coca-Cola had been reduced to an extremely small amount, then, although coca leaves were still used, all active cocaine was eliminated. Caffeine remains an ingredient, but interestingly, due to its bitterness, derivatives of the kola nut were also almost eliminated, meaning that the concoction no longer had any substantial amounts of the two ingredients that had gone into making its famous name!

By the 1930s, "Coke" was a part of American life. The "secret formula" for Coca-Cola has gone through more than a dozen alterations in its development, but the company has kept these changes quiet and jealously guarded the mystique of the formula. The existence of a lone copy of the original recipe, locked in a vault, is part of our nation's folklore. Coca-Cola's real secret was perhaps the ability to elevate a bottle of sugar and water into a national icon.

Toothpaste

What makes toothpaste?

Modern dentifrices (substances used for cleaning teeth, including toothpastes) contain a soft abrasive substance that works like scouring powder, glycerin to give body to the mixture, a detergent or soap as a cleaning agent, and a flavoring.

Just about half of most toothpastes are composed of tiny abrasive particles. Some toothpastes, like those used in many dental offices, are so gritty that you can feel it on your teeth. These particles help to remove daily deposits of plaque that accumulate on your teeth and gums. Since 1936, the American Dental Association (ADA) has rated baking soda as the least abrasive of all toothpastes. Baking soda kills bacteria, is inexpensive, and helps to neutralize the acids in the mouth which attack and weaken the teeth. However, baking soda has a salty and bitter taste and does not contain fluoride.

According to the ADA, one important criteria when selecting a toothpaste for children is to choose one that tastes good. The better it tastes, the more likely kids will brush! Also, the ADA recommends that the toothpaste contain fluoride, an ingredient said to make a major difference in preventing tooth decay. And third, they recommend checking for the seal of approval from the ADA.

Commercial toothpastes contain similar ingredients to those used in this *Secret Formulas* teacher's guide. Colgate and Tom's of Maine both supplied us with a list of ingredients—see the table on the next page for a comparison of these brands with our formula.

Toothpaste Ingredients

Secret Formulas	Tom's of Maine	Colgate	Purpose and/or Effect
N/A	sodium monofluorophosphate	sodium monofluorophosphate	active ingredient decay prevention
calcium carbonate	calcium carbonate	dicalcium phosphate dihydrate	mild abrasive
glycerin	glycerin	glycerin	moistener, smooth texture
water	water	water	consistency
powdered soap	sodium lauryl sulfate (from lauryl alcohol, derived from coconut oil)	sodium lauryl sulfate	calcium dispersant (Tom's) cleaning, foaming (Colgate)
N/A	carrageenan (seaweed)	cellulose gum	thickener
vanilla, lemon juice, mint	cinnamon, peppermint oils with other natural flavors	"flavor"	flavor
N/A	N/A	tetrasodium pyrophosphate	stabilizer
N/A	N/A	sodium saccharin	sweetener

Note: Tom's also states that its toothpaste contains no saccharin or artificial sweeteners, no preservatives, no artificial color or flavor, and no animal ingredients.

Regarding Calcium Carbonate

The abrasive ingredient, calcium carbonate, is used in our secret formula for toothpaste and in the toothpaste produced by Tom's of Maine. Calcium carbonate ($CaCO_3$) can be found in a variety of forms. In nature, it is found as limestone, marble, and in the mineral calcite. In your classroom and homes, it is found in chalk and eggshells. We use it in toothpaste for its abrasive property as a cleaner, but it also has some interesting chemical properties. Calcium carbonate reacts with acids to neutralize them in a chemical reaction. When it reacts, you can see bubbles form from the gas produced in the neutralization reaction. More commonly this reaction is used to relieve heartburn caused by excess stomach acid, so calcium carbonate is the main ingredient in many antacid tablets. That is why grinding up TUMS is one option for obtaining calcium carbonate.

When purchasing calcium carbonate for use in toothpaste, check the grade carefully. You want a product that is food grade—the powder's label should include the letters F.C.C. for Food Chemical Code, indicating that it has been packaged under conditions allowing its use in dietary supplements, yeast foods, etc. The container will also contain a warning regarding prolonged exposure to the dust from the powdered calcium carbonate. Prolonged exposure can cause irritation to the eyes, skin, mucous membranes, or kidneys. Be aware of this, if you plan to pour out large quantities. The "heavy" version of F.C.C. calcium carbonate powder (we list a source for this in the "Sources for Materials" section) will work well in the activities and will also probably reduce this potential dust problem.

Brief History of Toothpaste

Tooth care throughout history has been a mix of creative approaches and complete neglect. Those who neglected their teeth lost them at an early age or ended up with badly discolored teeth like those of Queen Elizabeth I. Ancient Egyptians used false teeth. They also used fillings, repairing cavities in decayed teeth with gold and enamel. The Romans brushed their teeth, but also relied on false teeth. The ancient Welsh kept their teeth clean by rubbing them often with a stick of green hazel covered with a woolen cloth.

Many substances have been used throughout history to clean teeth. Some of these dentifrices include: ground chalk, ground charcoal, powdered pumice stone, soap, lemon juice, ashes, and tobacco mixed with honey. During the sixteenth century a mixture called Vaughan's Water was used. It contained vinegar, pine tar, cinnamon and other spices, water, and honey.

A dental cream was produced in 1877 by the soap company, William Colgate & Company. As a marketing technique, it was repackaged in 1896 in a tube. This proved to be very popular! Americans really took to the use of toothpaste after World War II, when soldiers serving in the armed services brought the tooth brushing habit home. The brushing habit has intensified with greater social awareness of health issues, not to mention the onslaught of television advertising!

Ice Cream

What is ice cream?

Ice cream is a blend of dairy products, sugar, flavoring, sometimes eggs, federally approved additives, and air. Without air, ice cream would be an icy lump. Shaking and/or stirring helps make sure the air gets in! Commercial ice cream also contains stabilizers. Stabilizers, gelatins, and vegetables (such as carrageenan from seaweed, sometimes called Irish moss, and oat or guar gum) are used to prevent ice crystals from forming and to improve the ice cream's thickness and texture.

What does rock salt do?

When water is cooled to 0°C, it becomes a solid, which we know as ice. The formation of ice occurs because energy is removed from the liquid water as the temperature is lowered. When enough energy is removed, the water turns into a rigid solid because the water molecules no longer have enough energy to move and thus become fixed in place. This conversion from liquid to solid occurs at 0°C for water and is called the freezing point. At temperatures above the freezing point, water exists as a liquid, while at temperatures below the freezing point it exists as a solid. If both ice and liquid water are present (as in a glass of water containing ice cubes), then the temperature is exactly 0°C.

If you add rock salt to the water, it dissolves to form a salt solution (salty water). This causes the freezing point to be lowered by from 5–10 degrees. In other words, as the temperature of the rock salt solution is lowered to 0°C, ice does not form. If enough rock salt is added, the temperature must be lowered to -5°C, or even lower, in order to form ice. Therefore, if you have both ice and a solution containing rock salt, then the temperature is less than 0°C. If you place a ziplock bag containing pure water into this ice/rock salt solution, ice will form in the bag because the temperature of the ice/rock salt mixture is less than 0°C.

One way to understand why the temperature needs to be lower to form ice from a solution containing rock salt, compared to pure water, is as follows. At the freezing point, the rate at which water molecules leave the ice and enter the liquid is equal to the rate at which the water molecules leave the liquid and deposit onto the ice. Since these rates are equal, both liquid and solid exist. Addition of rock salt does not change the rate at which water molecules leave the ice and enter the liquid. However, the presence of rock salt in the liquid "blocks" some of the water molecules in the liquid from reaching the ice. More energy must be removed by lowering the temperature in order to overcome this interference caused by the presence of the rock salt.

Any substance (salt, sugar, etc.) that dissolves in water will lower the freezing point. Rock salt has a particularly large effect. This is why it is more difficult to freeze the salt water in oceans, compared to fresh water in lakes. It is also why rock salt is used to de-ice roads. You can try this by taking a piece of ice at 0°C and sprinkling salt on it. Watch closely as the ice melts.

Brief History of Ice Cream

Ice cream first developed from the process of chilling juices and wines, which led to early water ices and then to chilled concoctions containing milk and cream. The Greeks, Romans, and peoples of Palestine were familiar with wine cooled with snow and ice. Alexander the Great, during the siege of Petra, had thirty trenches filled with snow and covered with branches so that his ladies would have cool refreshment. The first known use of a substance resembling ice cream occurred during the rule of Nero Claudius Caesar (A.D. 54–68). He sent runners into the mountains for snow, which was relayed back to his table and flavored with honey, juices, and fruit pulp. At the end of thirteenth century, Marco Polo returned from the Far East with a recipe for a frozen dessert that included milk. The popularity of sherbets and ices grew in Italy and probably evolved into ice cream sometime in the sixteenth century. Ice cream was brought to the masses in 1670 with the opening of the first Parisian coffeehouse, the Cafe Procope.

Mistakes that Worked

Post-it Notes: A worker in the 3M research laboratories in 1970 was trying to find a new strong adhesive. Spencer Silver developed a new adhesive, but it was less strong than previously developed products. It stuck to objects, but was easily lifted off. Four years later another 3M scientist was singing in his church's choir and found that the markers he used to keep his place in the hymnal kept falling out. He coated the markers with the adhesive developed by Silver and that was the beginning of the Post-it note!

Velcro: Although people have been annoyed for hundreds of years by the burrs that stick to their clothing, it took until 1948 for someone to turn that experience into a brilliant and creative invention. George de Mestral, a Swiss engineer, returned from a walk and found cockleburs clinging to his cloth jacket. After examining a burr under a microscope he found it to be made up of small hooks that stick to clothing and fur. He experimented for eight years and then developed the interlocking structures on the two strips of nylon fabric we now call "hook and loop fastener" or "velcro" which has thousands of uses today.

Ivory Soap: In 1878, Procter & Gamble Company had developed "White Soap" a high quality soap which sold at an affordable price. One day a factory worker who was supervising the production went to lunch and forgot to turn off the mixing solution. As a result more air than usual was whipped into the soapy solution. Rather than throw away the mixture, the worker put it into the hardening frames to make bars of soap. Lo and behold, because of the air whipped into the soap, the soap bars floated! Consumer reaction was so favorable that Procter & Gamble immediately ordered that all their soap, which would soon be named "Ivory," should have air mixed into it.

Resources

Paste

Home and Workshop Guide to Glues and Adhesives, George Daniels, Harper and Row, New York, 1979.

Glue It!, Drs. Carl and Barbara Giles, Tab Books Inc., Blue Ridge Summit, Pennsylvania, 1984.

The Secret Life of School Supplies, Vicki Cobb, J.B. Lippincott, New York, 1981.

Cola

The Unsung Heroes, Nathan Aaseng, Lerner Publications, Minneapolis, 1989.

Secret Formula, Frederick Allen, HarperCollins, New York, 1994.

For God, Country and Coca-Cola: The Unauthorized History of the Great American Soft Drink and the Company That Makes It, Mark Pendergrast, Scribner's, New York, 1993.

Soda Pop, Arlene Erlbach, Lerner Publications, Minneapolis, 1994.

Toothpaste

The Secret Life of Cosmetics, Vicki Cobb, J.B. Lippincott, New York, 1985.

Protecting Our Children's Teeth, Malcolm S. Foster, D.D.S., Plenum Publishing Corporation, New York, 1992.

Brush, Comb, Scrub: Inventions to Keep You Clean (first published as *Keeping Clean*), Vicki Cobb, HarperCollins, New York, 1993.

Ice Cream

The Great Ice Cream Book, Paul Dickson, Atheneum, New York, 1973.

Ice Cream, William Jaspersohn, Macmillan, New York, 1988.

The Scoop on Ice Cream, Vicki Cobb, Little, Brown and Co., Boston, 1985.

Scoop After Scoop: A History of Ice Cream, Stephen Krensky, Atheneum, New York, 1986.

The Milk Makers, Gail Gibbons, Macmillan, New York, 1985.

Milk from Cow to Carton (first published as *Green Grass and White Milk*), Aliki, HarperCollins, New York, 1992.

Invention

Mistakes That Worked, Charlotte Foltz Jones, Doubleday, New York, 1991.

Small Inventions That Make A Big Difference, National Geographic Society, Washington, D.C., 1984.

Why Didn't I Think of That? From Alarm Clocks to Zippers, Webb Garrison, Prentice Hall, Englewood Cliffs, New Jersey, 1977.

The Invention of Ordinary Things, Don L. Wulffson, Lothrop, Lee and Shepard Books, New York, 1981.

Better Mousetraps: Product Improvements That Led to Success, Nathan Aaseng, Lerner Publications, Minneapolis, 1990.

The Rejects: People and Products That Outsmarted the Experts, Nathan Aaseng, Lerner Publications, Minneapolis, 1989.

The Fortunate Fortunes: Business Successes That Began with a Lucky Break, Nathan Aaseng, Lerner Publications, Minneapolis, 1989.

The Problem Solvers, Nathan Aaseng, Lerner Publications, Minneapolis, 1989.

General Reference

The Formula Manual, Stark Research Associates, Andrews and McMeel, Kansas City, Kansas, 1980.

Panati's Extraordinary Origins of Everyday Things, Charles Panati, Harper and Row, New York, 1989.

Gobs of Goo, Vicki Cobb, J.B. Lippincott, New York, 1983.

Chemistry Around You: Experiments and Projects with Everyday Products, Salvatore Tocci, Prentice Hall, New York, 1985.

Science and Serendipity, D.S. Halacy, Jr., Macrae Smith, Philadelphia, Pennsylvania, 1967.

Sources for Materials

Stick-On (Self-Adhesive) Dots for Color Coding

These are available at most stationery, office supply, and paper goods stores, as well as many grocery and drug stores. One of the leading manufacturers, Avery, calls them "Color Coding Labels" and makes $^3/_4$, $^1/_2$, and $^1/_4$ inch diameter dots. Any of these diameters is fine for these activities. Often these labels are sold in packages of only one color, in which case you will have to obtain enough different colors for the activities. Some companies do produce packages with multiple colors in them.

Trays

Trays are available at many restaurant supply stores and large discount stores. They can also be obtained, in varying colors, from scientific suppliers, such as VWR Scientific Products, Nasco, and others.

Cups

The wide-mouthed, "squat" cups recommended for these activities (9-ounce, Solo cups) are available at most supermarkets and many discount outlets.

Medicine Droppers

If you choose to obtain actual medicine droppers (rather than using the half-straw model) they are available from scientific supply companies. Fisher Scientific, for example, carries disposable pipets ($26 for 500 at time of this publication) or washable ones ($23 for 144). Their number is (800) 766-7000.

Spoons

As mentioned in the section on creating a basic kit for these activities, we recommend the smaller, more lightweight plastic spoons. They are available in many stores, including grocery and wholesale goods stores, as well as large discount outlets.

Calcium Carbonate

As noted in several places in this guide, one way to obtain the calcium carbonate needed for the toothpaste activities is to grind up TUMS tablets. TUMS of course are available at most grocery and drug stores.

Calcium carbonate in powder form is available from many chemical supply houses. Many suppliers, however, may not carry the food grade calcium carbonate (F.C.C. for Food Chemical Code) needed for these activities, or may not sell to individuals.

We have found at least one source for calcium carbonate that is able to supply food grade calcium carbonate directly to teachers for use in these activities. Please let us know if you find others. This source is:

Chem Lab Supplies
1060-C Ortega Way   or   13814 Inglewood Avenue
Placentia, CA 92670   Hawthorne, CA 90250
(714) 630-7902   (310) 973-2391

The item number is C1077, calcium carbonate, heavy powder, F.C.C. Prices at the time of this publication are $14.45 for 1 pound or $49.80 for 5 pounds; larger amounts are also sold. If, when ordering from Chem Lab Supplies, you mention that you are a teacher and that the calcium carbonate you are ordering is being used for making toothpaste in the Lawrence Hall of Science GEMS classroom activities, you can obtain a 10% discount.

If a school or school district, rather than an individual, is ordering, calcium carbonate can also be ordered from Spectrum Chemical Manufacturing Corporation. Please contact them directly for ordering information. The item number at Spectrum is also C1077. Spectrum Chemical operators can also provide you with names of suppliers in your region who will take individual orders. The number for Spectrum Chemical is (800) 772-8786.

Please understand that these suppliers are listed here as possible sources for the calcium carbonate needed in the toothpaste activities. While we have been told that the food grade powder is the same exact substance a toothpaste company would order for making its products, we cannot be held responsible for any variations in quality, issues of classroom handling, or other safety issues (see the note about prolonged exposure to dust on page 106 of "Behind the Scenes"). This is a generally safe substance, as evidenced by its use in TUMS. If you need more information, contact a supplier yourself, and, if you still have concerns, you may prefer to grind up TUMS so you have control over the process.

Popsicle Sticks

Packages of these are generally available in hobby/craft shops and art supply stores.

Ceramic Tiles

These are available from many large hardware stores, stores that specialize in tiles, as well as ceramic supply houses. It is often possible to arrange a donation of these from a tile store, especially of lines they are discontinuing, etc. The backs of the tiles need to be porous and white; the color/design on the front is unimportant for the activity. These tiles can be reused in subsequent classes.

Dear Parents,

Your child's class will soon begin a unit called *Secret Formulas*. Students will act as laboratory scientists as they develop their own "products." They will observe and test ingredients, then create and/or record their own personal formulas for paste, toothpaste, cola, and ice cream! In the process, they will learn important science skills and concepts and experience the actual work of science. This program was developed by the Great Explorations in Math and Science (GEMS) program at the Lawrence Hall of Science and tested in classrooms nationwide.

If any of you are able to volunteer an hour or two of your time to assist during presentation of this very hands-on unit it would be of invaluable assistance! There are also many materials that we need for this motivating unit, so we are asking for your help. Please see if you have any of the following items to donate, or if you know of others who do. Any items crossed out have already been gathered. Except for the milk and ice, listed separately below, we will need the materials by_____.

Thank you very much!

Non-Consumables

- ❒ 8 cafeteria trays
- ❒ 108 (9 dozen) clear, plastic cups 8 to 10 ounces
- ❒ about 10 dozen self-adhesive colored dots—two dozen each: red, blue, yellow, green, and orange. Any diameter of dot is fine.
- ❒ 48 small, lightweight plastic spoons (about $1/2$ teaspoon size)
- ❒ 32 plastic spoons (any size—for eating ice cream)
- ❒ about 36 plastic stirrers
- ❒ about 72 popsicle sticks (32 of these are consumable)
- ❒ 8 containers (cottage cheese-type, about 1 pint)
- ❒ 1 wide-tipped, black permanent felt marker
- ❒ 4 permanent markers (one each: yellow, green, blue, and orange)
- ❒ 2 sponges
- ❒ 1 pitcher, 2-quart capacity
- ❒ a one-teaspoon measuring spoon
- ❒ 1 measuring cup
- ❒ 1 spoon for blueberries
- ❒ 33 ceramic tiles, about 4" x 4" (the backs of the tiles are used for the activity, and need to be porous and white. The color on the front of the tiles doesn't matter.)
- ❒ 2 buckets or dishpans to be used for rinsing and dumping. One needs to be big enough to hold 32 tiles.
- ❒ 8 T-shirts (adult-sized)
- ❒ (*optional*) 1 cooler for the ice cubes
- ❒ (*optional*) 32 washable medicine droppers. If the class has these, the drinking straws listed under consumables are not needed.

Consumables

- ❐ 1 roll of plastic wrap
- ❐ 14 dozen ziplock sandwich bags
- ❐ 12 one-gallon size ziplock **freezer** bags
  (the Glad brand works well)
- ❐ 60 plastic drinking straws (unwrapped, not the kind that bend) *or* 120
  disposable medicine droppers
- ❐ about 12 dozen 3-oz. paper cups ("bathroom refill" type, but not the
  kind with pleated sides)
- ❐ 48 flat toothpicks
- ❐ 16 cotton swabs
- ❐ 8 sponges (each to be cut in 4 pieces for scrubbing)
- ❐ 10 lbs. of white, granulated sugar
- ❐ 2 lbs. of white flour
- ❐ 2 boxes (about 16 oz.) each of: baking soda, table salt, cornstarch
- ❐ 32 dried beans, uncooked, small, uniform size
  (black beans are fine)
- ❐ 6 lbs. of rock salt (about 8 cups)
- ❐ 8 small **squeeze** bottles of food coloring: three bottles red, three bottles
  blue, and two bottles yellow)
- ❐ 48 oz. of vanilla extract (imitation vanilla is fine)
- ❐ 16 oz. of lime juice
- ❐ 16 oz. of lemon juice
- ❐ 16 oz. of strawberry extract
- ❐ 16 oz. of mint extract
- ❐ 1 small container of ground cinnamon (about an ounce or a little less)
- ❐ 12 cans of club soda or salt-free, flavorless seltzer water
- ❐ three 12-oz. cans of cola (all the same brand)
- ❐ one small tube of toothpaste, any common brand (something not too
  strong tasting or "sting-y" is best; not one made with baking soda)
- ❐ about 300 TUMS tablets—regular flavor and color. *or* about three cups of
  calcium carbonate powder, food grade
- ❐ 2 cups of Ivory Snow laundry soap
- ❐ 1 tablespoon of bleach
- ❐ 12 oz. of glycerin (1 $^1/_2$ cups)
- ❐ 1 small can of blueberries

Perishable items needed near the day of the activity
(You'll get our schedule.)

- ❐ 1 gallon regular milk
- ❐ 20 lbs. of crushed ice (four 5-lb. bags) or ice cubes
- ❐ 1 bag of ice cubes (at least 1 cube per student) for cola session

Katrina   1. poured milk into my bag.   2. put bag into cup.

3. put in ingredients.   4. put bag in bigger bag

5. Shake.   6. Feel it.

7. Get spoon.   8. Eat!

Assessment Suggestions

Selected Student Outcomes

1. Students improve their ability to observe and compare substances and describe their attributes.

2. Students can predict that results are repeatable when the same exact procedure is followed.

3. Students can predict that certain ingredients will cause certain effects when mixed together to make something new and that those effects change when amounts of ingredients are changed, or when different ingredients are substituted.

4. Students improve their ability to keep careful records of their procedures.

5. Students improve their ability to measure level spoonfuls of dry ingredients and use a dropper.

6. Students use data they gather about ingredients to inform their decisions about what to put in their secret formulas.

7. Students gain insight into the ways scientific "experiments" and testing as well as creative inventiveness play a role in development of products we use daily.

Built-in Assessment Activities

• **Observing and Describing Attributes.** For each product that is explored (paste, cola, toothpaste, and ice cream), students are given opportunities to observe and describe the attributes, verbally in response to questions and also when they write their attribute riddles. The teacher can observe the quality of students descriptions and how this changes over the course of the unit. (Outcome 1)

• **Which is the Stickiest?** In Session 1, after concluding the Sticky Test, students are asked which "paste" mixture was the stickiest. Later in the session, after they've chosen ingredients to make their own "personal paste," they stick a square on a graph above the color of the ingredient they think is the stickiest. The teacher can assess students' understanding that a certain ingredient consistently causes stickiness. (Outcomes 1, 2, 3)

• **Which is the Sweetest?** In the first activity in Session 3, students taste mystery sugar waters and order them (by taste) according to most to least sweet. At the end of that activity, students are asked to make a statement about what effect sugar causes. In the second activity, students add sugar to their cups of water until the sweetness matches the sweetness of "cola water." At the end of the activity, students graph the results of their test. Observing students during these activities, and examining the graph that is produced can provide the teacher information about students' understanding of cause and effect and repeatability of results. (Outcomes 1, 2, 3)

• **Which is the Foamiest? The Best Cleaner?** At the end of Session 5 students are asked, based on a test they conducted, which ingredient caused the most foam. At the beginning of Session 6, students are asked which ingredient they would add to their toothpaste if they loved foamy toothpaste. The same is done in Session 6 with regard to which ingredients are the best cleaners, and what would they add to their toothpaste if they wanted a toothpaste that cleans really well. (Outcomes 2, 3, 6)

• **Repeatability.** At the end of Session 4, students are asked—"If you were to exactly follow your formula again, do you think your cola would turn out the same way?" The teacher can assess students' understanding of repeatability of results by asking this question at this time and at other key points in the unit. (Outcome 2)

• **Careful Record Keeping.** In making paste, students discover the need to record their secret formulas. In making cola, toothpaste, and then ice cream, students are given repeated opportunities to use and hone their record keeping skills. The teacher can observe whether students' data sheets improve over the course of the unit. (Outcome 4)

• **Mighty Measurers.** In the early sessions of the unit, students are shown how to measure level spoonfuls and use droppers. The teacher can observe how students' skills improve throughout the unit. (Outcome 5)

• **The Secrets Behind the Formulas.** In all of the activities in this unit, students gather data about the attributes of ingredients and make their own secret formula for a product. The teacher can observe to what extent students use information they discovered to inform their decisions about what to put in their secret formulas. For instance, after students discover the stickiest ingredient, do they decide to use that ingredient in their secret formula for paste? Students can be asked to explain why they decided to use the ingredients they did. (Outcome 6)

Additional Assessment Ideas

- **Advertisements.** As a Going Further activity after the cola sessions, students design an advertisement for cola. In this advertisement, students are asked to include a description of the attributes of their cola, the ingredient, as well as some of the data they collected. Students are invited to explain what caused their cola to be the way it is. Students could make advertisements for other products too. (Outcomes 1, 3, 6, 7)

- **Homemade Lemonade.** As a Going Further activity after the cola sessions, students make lemonade at home. They bring their secret lemonade formula back to class and explain why they chose what they did. (Outcomes 1, 3, 4, 6)

- **Making Ice.** As a Going Further activity after Session 8, students figure out how to freeze the bag of water that was in the cup of plain ice (and didn't freeze). The teacher can observe students' knowledge that rock salt mixed with ice causes water to freeze. (Outcome 3)

- **Watch and Predict.** Do something simple, such as blowing a bubble in the air and watching it float downward. Or dissolve a solid and watch it "disappear." After students have seen you do it, ask them to predict what might happen if you do it a second time. Do it a second time and then ask them to predict what might happen if you do it a third time. The teacher can see when students are convinced that an experiment repeated in exactly the same way will produce the same results. (Outcome 2)

- **Cause and Effect Game.** Present students with a scenario describing a "cause," (you lost your jacket on a cold day; you put your popsicle on a radiator; you forgot your homework; you made your mom a birthday card) and ask students to predict what the "effect" might be. Students could act out the "effect" or they could write, draw, or tell what it might be. (Outcome 3)

- **Paste Revisited.** As a Going Further activity at the end of the unit, students are invited to make a new formula for paste. They are asked to record their formula and how they arrived at it on a blank piece of paper. (Outcome 1, 3, 4, 5, 6)

- **Scientists at Work.** As a Going Further activity at the end of the unit, students brainstorm attributes of products and then ways that scientists might test for these attributes. Students draw a picture showing how scientists might test for the attributes of a favorite product. (Outcome 7)

• **Product Scientists.** As a Going Further activity at the end of the unit, product scientists (from industries in the community) are invited to come to class and describe how they use scientific tests to develop safe, useful products. Students could write a letter or make a comic strip explaining the role of the scientist in creating and testing new products. (Outcome 7)

• **Scientists at Work.** As a Going Further activity at the end of the unit, the class researches the history of post-its, velcro, or liquid soap (see "Behind the Scenes"). Students can share their discoveries orally, in a letter, or through a dramatized account. (Outcome 7)

Literature Connections

In selecting literature to accompany *Secret Formulas*, we sought books and stories that make meaningful connections to the underlying concepts embedded in the activities. For example, we sought books that provide insight into ingredients and mixtures, what happens when ingredients change, and the attributes of ingredients. The idea of cause and effect as a precursor to controlled experimentation is reflected in several books as are related ideas about inventiveness. You may also want to refer to the GEMS literature connections handbook, *Once Upon A GEMS Guide: Connecting Young People's Literature to Great Explorations in Math and Science*, which lists books according to science themes and mathematics strands, as well as by GEMS guide. We welcome your suggestions for other books to connect to *Secret Formulas*.

Arthur's Tooth
by Marc Brown
Little, Brown & Co., Boston. 1985
Atlantic Monthly Press, Boston. 1985
Grades: K–3

Arthur, the only one in his class who still has all his baby teeth, waits impatiently for his loose tooth to fall out. The illustrations, especially those of a dentist's office, emphasize healthy eating and snacking as well as proper dental health. Ties in to the toothpaste activities of the guide.

Bread and Jam for Frances
by Russell Hoban; illustrated by Lillian Hoban
Harper & Row, New York. 1964
Grades: Preschool–3

Frances sings "Jam on biscuits, jam on toast, jam is the thing that I like most" about her favorite food. She eats it to the exclusion of everything else for all three meals *and* snacks. However, after six servings in two days she has had enough. She finally realizes that too much of a good thing isn't good. Students may also discover this in Session 3 if they add too much sugar to water when matching the sweetness of cola water.

Brrr!
by James Stevenson
Greenwillow Books, New York. 1991
Grades: K–4

When his grandchildren complain about the cold weather, Grandpa recalls a cold winter from his childhood. Through the story Grandpa tells, this book presents a nice discussion of snow, ice, and wind—a few of the attributes of cold winter weather. This book is particularly useful as a read-aloud while the class is waiting for their bags of water to freeze in Session 8. As a bonus, the book ends with everyone eating and enjoying ice cream!

Chameleon Was A Spy
by Diane Redfield Massie
HarperCollins, New York. 1979
Grades: 2–6

Chameleon is extremely good at camouflage and wants to be a spy. He is hired by the Pleasant Pickle Company to retrieve their secret formula which was stolen by a pickle scientist from the Perfect Pickle Company. In his role as a spy, Chameleon runs into quite a bit of trouble, but thanks to an observant girl and his clever color changing he is eventually successful in returning the secret formula. In a very playful way, this book emphasizes the need for recording a recipe and the importance of secrecy in competitive businesses like cola manufacturing.

Charlie and the Chocolate Factory
by Roald Dahl; illustrated by Joseph Schindelman
Alfred A. Knopf, New York. 1964
Penguin Books, New York. 1988
Grades: 4–6

This well-known, well-loved book connects particularly well to *Secret Formulas*. It is noted that Mr. Bucket, Charlie's father, works in a toothpaste factory, screwing caps on the tubes. More importantly, Willie Wonka has many marvelous concoctions—some already a success, some in the developmental stages—all products of a creative and inventive mind. It is said that he is so clever that "…he's invented a way of making chocolate ice cream so that it stays cold for hours and hours without being in the icebox." Mr. Wonka no longer has ordinary factory workers; he asked them all to leave for fear of spies who might try to steal his secret recipes. The book works best as a read-aloud—appropriate sections of it could even be read during the waiting period in Session 8 since the book relates well to the entire guide.

Doctor De Soto
by William Steig
Farrar, Straus and Giroux, New York. 1982
Grades: K–3

Doctor De Soto, a dentist mouse, does very good work on both small and large animals—except those with a taste for mice. When a fox comes in with a horrid toothache, the kind-hearted doctor and his wife first fix the tooth then develop a secret formula in order to stay alive! This book emphasizes well the importance of our teeth and their maintained good health through dental care *plus* the ingenuity of the De Sotos in devising a secret formula to outfox the fox. Because the doctor's secret formula glues the fox's mouth shut, the book connects to the paste as well as to the toothpaste activities in *Secret Formulas*. Newbery Honor Book. Readers may also be interested in the sequel, *Doctor De Soto Goes To Africa,* in which the kind doctor and his wife repair an elephant's tooth.

Einstein Anderson Science Sleuth
by Seymour Simon; illustrated by Fred Winkowski
Viking Press, New York. 1980
Penguin Books, New York. 1986
Grades: 3–7

This is a book of scientific riddles which Einstein Anderson solves after the reader is first challenged to do so. In the "Universal Solvent" chapter, Einstein Anderson's friend Stanley tries to convince him that the cherry soda-looking liquid he has invented will dissolve anything. Anderson, however, uses his scientific knowledge to dispute this claim. While this is the only chapter that directly connects to *Secret Formulas,* this book demonstrates real-life uses for scientific principles and will appeal to older students. It is recommended as a read-aloud for grades 1 to 3 and as an independent reader for third graders.

Freckle Juice
by Judy Blume; illustrated by Sonia O. Lisker
Dell Publishing, New York. 1971
Grades: 3–4

Andrew thinks that if he had as many freckles as a classmate, his mother would never know if the back of his neck was dirty. Though it costs five weeks of allowance, he buys Sharon's secret recipe for freckles (the recipe is given in the book). When Andrew mixes all the ingredients in a glass, he adds ice because "all drinks tasted better cold." Also, he starts with just one glassful. He'll drink another if he wants more freckles, but doesn't want to overdo it the first time. The attributes of some of the freckle juice ingredients are briefly mentioned and cause and effect is an overall theme of the book. This is a good early chapter book, especially appropriate for third graders and could be read aloud to students in lower grades.

Frog and Toad Are Friends
by Arnold Lobel
Harper & Row, New York. 1970
Grades: K–2

This book contains five tales recounting the adventures of two best friends—Frog and Toad. In the story "A Lost Button," Toad loses a button from his jacket. In trying to find it, he and Frog discuss the attributes of the lost button. This story ties in well to the entire guide's focus on attributes. Caldecott Honor Book.

Gorky Rises
by William Steig
Farrar, Straus & Giroux, New York. 1980
Grades: 2–5

When Gorky's parents leave the house, he sets up a laboratory at the kitchen sink and mixes up a concoction with a few secret ingredients—his mother's perfume and his father's cognac! The liquid proves to have magical properties which allow him to float high above the ground. In addition to the "mixing ingredients" aspect of this book, cause and effect also play a role in the story. Because of its connection to the whole guide, this is an appropriate book to read during the waiting period in Session 8. Your class could discuss the fact that Gorky doesn't carefully measure or record his ingredients and therefore probably can't recreate his formula. Although it is a picture book, the content makes it usable for older students.

Ice Cream Soup
by Frank Modell
Greenwillow Books, New York. 1988
Grades: Preschool–3

Two friends, Martin and Marvin, plan to give themselves a birthday party. Making the invitations and decorations goes well, but making the cake and ice cream proves difficult. After doing the ice cream activities in Sessions 8 and 9, students will understand what Martin and Marvin neglected to do when making their ice cream.

Indian in the Cupboard
by Lynne Reid Banks
Avon, New York. 1982
Grades: 3–7

In this well known story, nine-year-old Omri receives a plastic Indian, a cupboard, and its key for his birthday. He becomes involved in an adventure when the Indian comes to life and befriends him. It is the early chapters of the book, where Omri figures out how the cupboard works, that connect best with *Secret Formulas*. After noticing that the plastic Indian came to life after having been in the cupboard, Omri must experiment to find the correct sequence of events which bring the Indian to life—a great example of cause and effect. A drawback of the book is its stereotypical portrayal of Indians.

June 29, 1999
by David Wiesner
Clarion Books/Houghton Mifflin, New York. 1992
Grades: 1–6

The science project of Holly Evans takes an extraordinary turn—or does it? This highly imaginative and humorous book has a central experimental component, and conveys the sense of unexpected results. Holly is a careful and wise scientist—when she realizes that her experiment has failed, she is more curious than disappointed and she asks questions. The need to record data from an experiment (as students must keep track of ingredients put in their secret formulas) is a pretty strong message in the book. Since Holly keeps records on the vegetables she floats into the ionosphere, she is able to figure out that the falling veggies are not hers. In one illustration, there is a clipboard and map in the background on which Holly is keeping track of the vegetables that have fallen and where. Also, look carefully at the illustration where Holly is presenting her experiment to her class. Near her poster you can see a jar of Secret Plant Food and several jars of ingredients. Because of its emphasis on evidence versus inference as well as cause and effect, this book ties in well with the entire *Secret Formulas* guide.

Look! Snow!
by Kathryn O. Galbraith; illustrated by Nina Montezinos
Macmillan Publishing, New York. 1992
Grades: Preschool–2

This nearly wordless picture book conveys the joy and excitement of the season's first snowfall—feelings shared by school children, their teacher, and their bus driver. While other books illustrate the trouble snow can cause, the physical reasons snow occurs, or the things one can do in snow, this book simply celebrates snow. Most appropriate for young readers, it is recommended for the strong feelings it conveys so well.

Samuel Todd's Book of Great Inventions
by E. L. Konigsburg
Atheneum, New York. 1991
Grades: Preschool–2

Samuel Todd points out the many useful inventions that improve every day of our lives. The inventions are common items such as velcro, backpacks, thermos bottles, and stepstools. This is a picture book and may not be appropriate for the upper grade levels of *Secret Formulas*. The best quality of the book is that it reminds us that even everyday items—like mirrors—did not exist at one time.

The Snowy Day
by Ezra Jack Keats
Viking Press, New York. 1962
Grades: Preschool–2

This is the classic story about the adventures of a young boy on a snowy day. He plays in the snow in many different ways. At the end of the day, Peter learns something important about snow. The book ties in with the water freezing activities of Session 8. Caldecott Award Book.

Stone Soup
by Marsha Brown
Charles Scribner's Sons, New York. 1947
Grades: K–3

Three hungry soldiers come marching into a French village in search of a bit of food. Not until the soldiers begin to make a pot of stone soup do the peasants of the village slowly share their food. Each family contributes a bit of vegetable, meat, grain, milk, or spice to make a soup that the whole village sits down to eat. A negative aspect of the book is the way the peasants hide their food from the approaching soldiers and the way the soldiers trick the peasants into sharing. But in the end all benefit from the situation with a good meal, and the peasants learn a valuable lesson. The book could lead to a discussion about the contribution each separate ingredient makes to a whole product.

The Toothpaste Millionaire
by Jean Merrill; illustrated by Jan Palmer
Houghton Mifflin, Boston. 1972
Grades: 2–8

In *Secret Formulas* students develop and manufacture toothpaste. This book talks about the next step—selling and marketing it. Incensed by the price of a tube of toothpaste, twelve-year-old Rufus tries making his own from bicarbonate of soda with peppermint or vanilla flavoring. Rufus doesn't start out to become a millionaire—just to make inexpensive toothpaste. Assisted by his friend Kate and his math class (which becomes known as Toothpaste 1), his company grows from a laundry room operation to a corporation with stocks and bank loans. Unfortunately the book doesn't speak extensively on the development of the toothpaste recipe or on cause and effect. Most of the book is about how the business grows and about marketing, packaging, and shipping the toothpaste. Throughout the book are many opportunities to use math thus making it ideal to illustrate the need for, and use of, mathematics in the context of real-world problem solving. The math problems presented in the book are higher than the third grade level, but could be brought down to the appropriate grade level. This book is most useful as a read-aloud for first through third graders.

Two Bad Ants
by Chris Van Allsburg
Houghton Mifflin, Boston. 1988
Grades: Preschool–4

When an ant colony following their scout finds the source of the beautiful sparkling crystals (sugar) their queen desires, two adventurous ants separate themselves from the colony in order to remain in the sugar bowl. Unfortunately their decision to stay in the strange environment proves perilous. Finally they decide to return to the safety of their colony. As the two bad ants found out, an abundance of sugar is not necessarily a good thing. Students may find the same is true if they add too much sugar to their water when matching the sweetness of cola water in Session 3.

Ups and Downs with Oink and Pearl
by Kay Chorao
Harper & Row, New York. 1986
Grades: K–3

This book contains two stories starring Oink and Pearl, brother and sister piglets. In the first story "Super-Fizz Soda," Oink makes a super-fizz ice-cream soda as a birthday gift for Pearl. Lacking the key ingredient, soda water, Oink substitutes baking soda and lemon juice. These give the same bubbly effect, but drastically alter the taste and texture of the drink. In the end, Oink and Pearl have a good laugh over the silliness of the soda. This is an easy-reader book that students could read to themselves.

Vegetable Soup
by Jeanne Modesitt; illustrated by Robin Spowart
Macmillan, New York. 1988
Grades: Preschool–2

A husband and wife rabbit are about to have their first lunch in their new home, but their carrot sack is empty. They decide to borrow some carrots from their animal neighbors but can find none. Each neighbor does however have a different vegetable to offer, and the rabbits, still hoping for carrots, unwillingly accept their offerings. Realizing they won't be able to have carrots for their lunch, they decide to combine all the other vegetables they have into a soup. This book introduces the idea that individual ingredients can combine to form a better whole and can be used as a way to introduce ingredients in Session 1.

Water's Way
by Lisa Westberg Peters; illustrated by Ted Rand
Arcade Publishing, New York. 1991
Grades: K–3

"Water has a way of changing" inside and outside Tony's house,
from clouds to steam to fog and other forms. Innovative
illustrations show the changes in the weather outside while
highlighting water changes inside the house. This book clearly
describes the phase changes of water. An ideal book to read
aloud while students are waiting for their bags of water to freeze
in Session 8.

Preparation Checklists and Summary Outlines

Creating Your Basic *Secret Formulas* Kit

Getting Ready
____ 1. Assemble materials listed on page 10 for the "basic kit."
____ 2. Label the "personal" cups with initials marking the three-ounce point.
____ 3. Color code a set of ingredient cups for each group:
  • two red-dot cups (two cups, each with one red dot)
  • one blue-dot cup
  • one yellow-dot cup
  • one green-dot cup
  • one orange-dot cup
  • one **half**-dot yellow cup
  • one **half**-dot green cup
____ 4. Cut straws in half for use as droppers.
____ 5. Ask for volunteer help and material donations for the unit.
____ 6. Plan how to obtain calcium carbonate for the toothpaste activities, either by grinding up TUMS or ordering powdered calcium carbonate.

Session 1: What Makes Paste?

Getting Ready
Before the Day of the Activity
____ 1. Decide if you'll pre-teach the water-dropper technique.
____ 2. Plan room arrangement for groups of four.

On the Day of the Activity
Materials On Trays
____ 1. Fill ingredient cups half full and set on trays.
____ 2. Add plastic spoons, popsicle sticks, and droppers to cups.
____ 3. Color code four paper cups per group.
____ 4. Add a few damp paper towels to each tray.
____ 5. Set out the trays and demonstration materials.

Materials Not on Trays
____ 1. Make color-code key for class.
____ 2. Prepare class bar graph.
____ 3. Cut paper squares for bar graph.
____ 4. Cut scratch paper or gather 3" x 5" cards for the sticky test.
____ 5. Keep handy: scratch paper, paper squares, pencils, beans, extra paper cups, sponges, newspaper, ziplock bags.

Introducing the Activity

1. Ask if students ever made a secret potion or secret formula. Define "ingredients."
2. Say each group will mix four different powders with water to see which makes best paste.
3. Explain color-coded key, and introduce color-coded cups of ingredients.
4. Tell students to observe powders, but no eating or tasting.
5. Demonstrate adding powders:
   - Say each student will test **one** of the four powders.
   - Show how to measure two level spoonfuls of powder into paper cup.
6. Demonstrate the water-dropper technique.
7. Have class practice with imaginary droppers: **squeeze, unsqueeze, squeeze.**
8. Show how to add a few squirts of water to powder, stir with popsicle stick, observe.
9. Ask, "What does paste need to be like so you'd want to use it?" [Be sure someone mentions stickiness.]
10. Ask each student to observe their mixture, then pass cups around in their group.

Conducting the Ingredient Tests

1. Have teams get materials and begin.
2. Circulate, helping students use droppers.
3. Give a two-minute warning to finish up. Circulate, asking students to think of good words to describe mixtures.
4. Groups stop, set down materials. Ask, "What did you notice?" "Were any of the mixtures sticky?" "Did you notice any smell?" "How did they feel?" etc.

Explaining the Sticky Test

1. Students will test how well a bean sticks to paper (or card) using each of their four mixtures.
2. Demonstrate how to put small dab on paper or card.
3. Explain they'll lift papers all at same time. Ask for predictions.
4. Have students get materials and begin.

Conducting the Sticky Test

1. When the class is ready, have them lift their papers.
2. If necessary, have students wave or gently shake their papers.
3. Ask class to set down materials. Summarize class results by a show of hands.
4. Have a student collect all the used paper cups.

Making Your "Personal Paste"

1. Each student will get new paper cup, and may mix more than one ingredient.

2. Explain limit of **five powder spoonfuls.** They can use as many squirts of water as they need.

3. Have them begin. When a group finishes, collect all materials except personal paste cups.

Graphing the Stickiest Ingredients and Cleaning Up

1. Before cleaning up, regain attention of class.

2. Students vote on which ingredient was the stickiest, while cleaning up.

3. Show how to put a paper square on the graph, **using their own paste.**

4. Go over clean up procedures.

5. Pass out paper squares; students add squares to graph and clean up.

6. As students finish, give them ziplock bags. Have them store pastes to take home.

7. Ask for observations about the graph.

8. Wash and rinse cups and spoons—air dry.

Session 2: Tasting and Describing Cola

Getting Ready
___ Refrigerate cans of cola.

Telling Attribute Riddles

1. Say that you're thinking of something people can drink.

2. Give hints, asking a student to make a guess after each hint.

3. Play once or twice more. Say that all hints you gave are **attributes.**

4. Ask students for three attributes of grape juice. Write attributes on board as a riddle.

5. Continue creating "riddles" for one or two other familiar drinks (not cola yet).

Tasting and Describing Cola

1. Tell class they'll make secret formulas for cola later, but first they'll taste some real cola and think of attributes.

2. Pass out personal cups. Pour each student about half an inch of cola. Ask for attributes.

3. List "Attributes of Cola" and save for Session 4.

4. If students contribute ingredients, list them separately, under "Ingredients?"

5. Collect empty cups.

Writing a Cola Attribute Riddle
1. Say they will use three attributes to write a cola riddle for parents or friends to solve.
2. Work on one or two riddles together.
3. Have students write one or more riddles and take them home.

Session 3: Investigating an Ingredient of Cola

Getting Ready
(Prepare for Activity 2 first, then Activity 1)

For Activity 2: Matching the Sweetness of Cola
___ 1. In the pitcher, mix "cola water" for the orange-dot cups.
- Decide how many cups of cola water are needed for whole class.
- Mix three level measuring teaspoons of sugar per cup of water.
- Pour three ounces of cola water into orange-dot cup for each group.

___ 2. Put half-cup of dry sugar into each of two red-dot cups for each group. Place two small plastic spoons, two popsicle sticks, and two plastic stirrers in each cup.

___ 3. Put these materials on each group's tray:
- 1 orange-dot cup of cola water
- 2 red-dot cups with sugar, spoons, popsicle sticks, and stirrers
- 4 paper cups
- 4 pieces scratch paper
- 4 pencils

___ 4. Set aside trays.

For Activity 1: Mystery Sugar Waters
___ 1. In the pitcher, mix three other sugar water solutions:
- For the blue-dot cups: Mix 1 level measuring teaspoon of sugar per cup of water in pitcher.
- For the yellow-dot cups: Mix 3 level measuring teaspoons of sugar per cup of water in pitcher. (Same as cola water solution in Activity 2.)
- For the green-dot cups: Mix 6 level measuring teaspoons of sugar per cup of water in pitcher.

___ 2. Pour three ounces of each solution into the right cups.

___ 3. Keep track of which solution you put in each color-dot cup, but don't make a color-code chart.

___ 4. Have Activity 1 materials ready for distribution, but not on trays:
- all of the blue-, yellow-, and green-dot cups of solutions
- students' personal cups
- 1 dump container for each group

___ 5. Have teacher demonstration materials for Activity 1 handy:

- three unlabeled plastic cups, each with three ounces of plain water
- a cup half-full of sugar with a small plastic spoon, popsicle stick, and stirrer
- a pitcher of plain water

Mystery Sugar Waters: Introducing the Activity

1. Say one ingredient in most colas is sugar. They'll do two sugar-tasting activities.
2. Say you're going to add sugar to water and stir. Ask what will happen.
3. Put **one** level spoonful sugar into the first cup, **three** in second, and **six** in the third. Ask for predictions about sweetness.
4. Rearrange the cups. Ask, *"Now* how can we tell which mystery cup has one, three, or six spoonfuls of sugar?"

Tasting the Mystery Sugar Waters

1. Say that you made three cups just like these for each group. Which is which?
2. Demonstrate how to pour a little sip into their personal cup, and taste. Show how to pour out extra, and taste the sugar water from each of the other two mystery cups the same way.
3. Distribute materials, and have the class begin.
4. Collect all materials except personal cups. Ask which was sweet, sweeter, sweetest? Ask, "What can we say about adding sugar—what effect does it cause?"

Matching the Sweetness of Cola: Introducing the Activity

1. Hold up an orange-dot cup, and ask, "How many spoonfuls of sugar do you think might be in this much Classic Coke?"
2. Say that you got the sugar formula for Classic Coke, and used it to mix this sugar water that tastes as sweet as Classic Coke!
3. Say they'll each get a sample of this "cola water" in their group's orange-dot cup. Ask, "How could you find out how much sugar is in this cola water?"

Explaining the Procedure

1. Say there are paper cups for each student on tray for tasting cola water.
2. They'll each get plain water in their personal cup.
3. There are two red-dot cups of sugar on each tray. It is **not** okay to taste the dry sugar.
4. Each student writes "sugar" on piece of scratch paper. Each time they add one level spoonful to their personal cup, they make tally mark.
5. After each spoonful, they'll stir until they can't see the sugar any more, taste it, and then taste a sip of the "cola water" in their paper cup. Repeat until they match.
6. When their water is sweet enough, they should stop.

Experimenting and Graphing Results

1. Have student from each group get tray of materials. With pitcher, fill personal cups to 3 ounce level, and have them begin.
2. Circulate, reminding students to tally, taste between spoonfuls, and take small sips. Take sugar cups away from groups as they finish.
3. Have them put all materials on tray and have a student take tray to central location.
4. Write numbers 1 through 5 on chalkboard (or butcher paper) horizontally along a lower edge.
5. Poll class for results, making column of Xs above each number in graph. Have class summarize results.
6. Save graph and cups of sugar with spoons, popsicle sticks, and stirrers for Session 4.
7. Pour out sugar waters. Wash cups and air dry. Throw away paper cups. Have students wipe tables.

Session 4: Secret Formulas for Cola

Getting Ready

___ 1. Make a class color key for sugar, lime juice, vanilla, and cinnamon to match colors listed below.

___ 2. Mix 1 teaspoon red with a half teaspoon green food coloring to make brown—add a dropper.

___ 3. Add more sugar to red-dot cups so there is about half a cup of sugar in each.

___ 4. Put ingredients into color-coded cups. Place on tray:
  - 2 red-dot cups: sugar
  - green-dot cup: about $1/4$ cup of lime juice (2 ounces) with two droppers
  - yellow-dot cup: about $1/4$ cup of vanilla (2 ounces) with two droppers
    Place a piece of plastic wrap over vanilla cups to slow evaporation.
  - blue-dot cup: one teaspoon cinnamon with two toothpicks
  - 1 unopened can club soda (12 ounces)

___ 5. Have handy, **but not on trays:**
  - ice (in cooler if possible)
  - containers for ice
  - your personal cup
  - student personal cups
  - one Cola data sheet per student

Introducing the Ingredients

1. Ask the class about the paste they made. Why is it important to write down formulas?

2. Tell them for cola they will carefully record how much of each ingredient they use.

3. Introduce the new ingredients, using the class color key and ingredient cups.
   - Emphasize adding small amounts.
   - Tell them to add lime juice and vanilla one drop (not squirt) at a time.
   - Demonstrate wafting.
   - Demonstrate how to scoop cinnamon with toothpick.

4. Refer to Session 3 graph of sugar in cola water which might help to determine how much sugar to add now.

Demonstrating How to Make Your Own Cola

1. Each group will get one can of club soda. Each student will pour club soda into their cup until it touches the bottom of letters.

2. Add a few drops of brown food coloring to club soda in your cup. Explain that you will add brown coloring to their cans of club soda before they pour it.

3. Show data sheet. Model adding and recording different ingredients.

4. The sheet has only nine toothpick pictures for cinnamon because that is the **most** they can use.

5. Let them know they don't have to use all ingredients.

6. Encourage them to take little tastes. When they think their cola is perfect, they should raise their hands and you will bring ice to their group, which they may add to their cola.

7. (*Optional*) Have them color code the data sheet using color key as reference.

Let the Cola Making Begin!

1. Pass out trays, data sheets, and personal cups. Add about 10 drops of food coloring to each group's can of club soda. Have students begin.

2. Fill containers with 4–8 ice cubes each and distribute as groups finish.

3. Show students where to dump cola they don't like and where to put dirty cups. Collect trays. Have them keep Cola data sheets.

Discussing the Attributes of a Good Cola

1. Read list of attributes of cola brainstormed in Session 2, and have students give thumbs up (or down) if it describes their cola.

2. Ask students if they think their cola would turn out the same way if they were to follow their formula exactly again.

3. Are there any ingredients or amounts they would choose to change next time?

4. Explain that all the ingredients are easy to get at a grocery store so their secret formula can be made at home.

Session 5: Tasting, Describing, and Testing Toothpaste

Getting Ready
Before the Day of the Activity
___ Obtain calcium carbonate powder *or* grind about 300 TUMS tablets for the three toothpaste sessions. (About two-thirds of this powder is for Session 7.)

On the Day of the Activity
___ 1. Make a class color key:
- orange: calcium carbonate
- yellow: soap
- green: glycerin
- blue: water

___ 2. Put ingredients into cups on each tray:
- orange-dot cup: 2–3 tablespoons calcium carbonate powder (ground TUMS)
- yellow-dot cup: about $1/8$ cup Ivory Snow soap (one ounce)
- green-dot cup: about $1/4$ cup glycerin (two ounces)
- blue-dot cup: about $1/4$ cup water (two ounces)

___ 3. Add droppers, spoons, and popsicle sticks.

___ 4. Add four extra plastic cups to trays.

___ 5. Stick colored dots on bags, and sort so each group will have four different-colored bags.

___ 6. For each group, fill a container with water and put three-ounce paper cup in it to be a measurer/dipper.

___ 7. Squeeze dab of toothpaste onto a paper towel for each group. Have ready, with toothpicks, but **not on trays.**

Introducing Toothpaste
1. Announce that they'll be toothpaste scientists.
2. Ask, "Why do people brush their teeth?" "Why is brushing important after drinking cola?" "What does the brush do?"
3. Say their group will get a toothpaste dab. Show how to use a toothpick for tasting.

Tasting Toothpaste and Thinking of Attributes
1. Pass out toothpaste and toothpicks. Ask students to think of attributes.
2. Regain their attention. Ask for Attributes of Toothpaste—list on paper/chalkboard.
3. Ask what some of the ingredients might be.
4. Throw away toothpicks and toothpaste.

Making Attribute Riddles for Toothpaste

1. Tell students they will write toothpaste riddles using attributes, as with cola.
2. Remind them to use three attributes from the list, or any other attributes they think of. Practice on one or two riddles as a class.
3. Have students write their own riddle(s), and take home.

(If you want to make this session into two shorter sessions, end first part here.)

Introducing Four Toothpaste Ingredients

1. Briefly introduce ingredients, using the cups and the class color key.
2. Emphasize **no tasting in this session.**

Introducing the Feel Test

1. Say they'll do two tests to help them decide which ingredients to put in their secret formulas. Ask, "What does toothpaste feel like?"
2. Show how each person in group will add one of the ingredients to a plastic bag. The color dot on bag should match the ingredient they test.
3. Write the amounts they should use on the board (4 squirts glycerin, 4 squirts water, 1 level spoonful calcium carbonate, plus 2 squirts water, 1 level spoonful soap, plus 2 squirts water).
4. Remind them to level powders. Show how to feel ingredient through bag.
5. Ask them to notice what the ingredients feel like: watery/slimy, or thick/dry.

Introducing the Foam Test

1. Explain foam test by asking for thumbs up if they like foamy, bubbly toothpaste. Say they'll add more water and shake bags to test foaminess.
2. Show how to dip paper cup into water, and pour water into bag with ingredient already in it.
3. Show how to set the bag into a cup for stability, zip up the bag, then shake it.

Doing the Feel and Foam Tests

1. Remind students to do feel test first, then foam test. Distribute trays and water. Have groups begin.
2. For foam test, check seals on bags. Have extra bags handy in case of leaks.
3. When done, have students return trays and bags to central area, and wipe tables as necessary.

Discussing Results of the Tests
1. Tape color key to chalkboard and write "Foam Test" next to it. Record results by putting stars next to ingredients.
2. Ask class how each ingredient felt. Accept several answers for each ingredient.
3. Save trays of cups, color key, and record of foam test results.
4. Empty water containers. Throw away ziplock bags and paper cups.

Session 6: Testing More Toothpaste Ingredients

Getting Ready
Materials on Trays
___ 1. Replenish ingredient cups from Session 5. Check droppers, spoons, and popsicle sticks.
___ 2. Cut a sponge into four pieces for each group. Get sponges damp and add to trays.

Materials Not on Trays
___ 1. Use orange, yellow, green, and blue permanent markers to color code tiles. Stack four different-colored tiles for each group.
___ 2. Put spoonful of blueberries and two cotton swabs in paper cup for each team.
___ 3. Have ready for distribution after introduction: tile stacks, cups of blueberries, four paper towels per group.
___ 4. For your demonstration, have one tile, a paper towel, a cup of blueberries, and one of the trays of ingredients.
___ 5. Set up a rinse station. Fill a rinse tub half-full of water, and set a small pile of paper towels next to it.

Introducing the Cleaning Test
1. Briefly review findings from feel and foam tests. Help students think about cause and effect (more soap = foamier).
2. In this session they'll test the same ingredients to see which one cleans best.
3. Ask students for ideas, then hold up a tile, and tell them they will stain the tiles with blueberries, then see which ingredient scrubs it clean the best.

Staining the Tiles
1. Tell the students not to taste the blueberries.
2. Show how to set tile on paper towel shiny side down.
3. Demonstrate how to dip cotton swab into blueberries and make stain about as big as a quarter on middle of back of tile. Caution them about staining clothes and breaking tiles.
4. Pass out blueberries, paper towels, and tiles, but not trays yet. Have students make stains. Collect blueberries and swabs.

Explaining the Procedure for the Cleaning Test

1. Explain that each student in group will put one of four ingredients on tile. The colored dot in corner of their tile tells them what to put on. Later everyone will get to scrub all four tiles.
2. Demonstrate measuring ingredients:
    - glycerin or water: Squirt **two dropperfuls** on stain.
    - calcium carbonate or soap: Put **one level spoonful** on stain.
3. Ask: "What are we trying to find out?" [which ingredient cleans best]
4. Explain how they'll pass tiles around their group:
    - Scrub the tile they have now, while you count to 10.
    - Pass that tile and sponge to person on their right. Scrub for count of 10.
    - Repeat until they get their starting tile back.
5. Tell students not to start scrubbing until your signal.

Conducting the Cleaning Test

1. Pass out trays, and have the students put ingredients on tiles.
2. Give your signal. Do the counting-scrubbing-passing four times.
3. Have the class stop and wipe fingers. Ask one student from each group to rinse tiles.
4. Collect ingredients and sponges. Let groups compare their tiles.
5. Ask someone from each table to report their group findings. Record with stars on board under the heading "Cleaning Test."
6. Encourage them to think about cause and effect: "If you want a toothpaste to clean well, which ingredient(s) would you include?" Mention two other attributes of soap—tastes bad, slimy.
7. Collect the tiles and soak them in rinse tub.

Clean Up

1. Save trays with ingredient cups, spoons, popsicle sticks, and droppers for next session.
2. Save the color key of ingredients.
3. Soak and rinse sponges. Wipe tables.
4. Add a tablespoon of bleach to water in rinse tub. Soak tiles for a few hours or overnight. Quickly scrub and rinse.

Session 7: Secret Formulas for Toothpaste

Getting Ready
Materials on Trays

___ 1. If necessary, replenish ingredient cups, and check droppers, spoons, and popsicle sticks. Have on tray for each group:
  - orange-dot cup: 2–3 tablespoons of calcium carbonate powder (ground TUMS)
  - yellow-dot cup: about $1/8$ cup Ivory Snow soap (one ounce)
  - green-dot cup: about $1/4$ cup glycerin (two ounces)
  - blue-dot cup: about $1/4$ cup water (two ounces)

___ 2. Add new ingredient cups to trays for a total of seven:
  - red-dot cup: about $1/4$ cup vanilla extract (two ounces)
  - yellow **half**-dot cup: about $1/4$ cup lemon juice (two ounces)
  - green **half**-dot cup: about $1/4$ cup mint extract (two ounces)

___ 3. Put a dropper into each new cup.

___ 4. Cover the extract cups with plastic wrap to slow evaporation.

Materials Not on Trays

___ 1. Add the extra ingredients to your class color key so it now includes:
  - orange-dot: calcium carbonate
  - yellow-dot: soap
  - green-dot: glycerin
  - blue-dot: water
  - red-dot: vanilla
  - **half**-dot of yellow: lemon
  - **half**-dot of green: mint

___ 2. Write each student's initials on ziplock bag with permanent marker.

___ 3. Have personal cups handy (to set the bags in, for stability).

___ 4. Duplicate one Toothpaste data sheet per student. Gather crayons if students will color code data sheet.

Introducing the Activity
1. Ask if ingredients they choose will make a difference in attributes of their toothpaste.
2. Focus on consistency:
  - "Who likes slimy or watery toothpaste?" "Why not?"
  - "Which ingredient(s) would you add to make toothpaste dryer and thicker?"
  - "Which ingredient(s) would you add to make your toothpaste more squishy?"

3. Use class color key to introduce three new ingredients. Say they are all flavorings.
  - They can smell them before using. Review wafting.
  - They don't have to use all the flavors.
  - They'll add only a little of these strong flavors.

Modeling How to Add and Mix Ingredients
1. Show students the bags for mixing their toothpastes and taking them home.
2. Show how to set bag into personal cup so it won't tip over.
3. Model how to mix ingredients and check how the mixture feels.
4. Demonstrate how to measure a small scoop of soap with toothpick, and remind them how to make drops.

Modeling How to Record on the Data Sheet
1. Pass out data sheets. Have students color code ingredients (optional).
2. Show how to record added ingredients. Stress importance of careful record-keeping.
3. Explain there are **limits** to the amounts of ingredients that can be used.

Let the Toothpaste Making Begin!
1. Pass out ziplock bags and personal cups, and trays. Have them begin.
2. Circulate, checking that students are recording, and asking what they could add to make it more like commercial toothpaste.
3. Have students return trays of materials, keep bags of toothpaste, and wipe tables.
4. Have them seal bags to take their toothpaste home and test. (Say it's not food, and to keep it away from younger siblings.)

Session 8: Ice Cream Testing

Getting Ready
For Ice Cream Ingredients Demonstration
___ 1. Make a color key.
  - blue: sugar
  - green: vanilla
  - orange: strawberry

___ 2. Draw enlarged version of data sheet on chalkboard.

___ 3. Fill four ingredient cups for demonstration. (Don't prepare student ingredient cups until next session.)
  - blue: Half a cup of sugar, spoon, popsicle stick
  - green: $1/4$ cup (2 ounces) vanilla extract and dropper (Cover with plastic wrap.)
  - orange: $1/4$ cup (2 ounces) strawberry extract and dropper (Cover.)
  - your personal cup with milk to the bottom of initials (3 ounces) and stirrer

___ 4. Set up your demonstration materials.
- Three cups of ingredients
- Your personal cup of milk
- Empty ziplock bag with your initials
- Three squeeze bottles food coloring (red, yellow, blue)

For the Ice and Rock Salt Activity
___ 1. Fill two ziplock bags per group with about a tablespoon of water each, and seal them.
___ 2. Choose a storybook to read during the session.
___ 3. Set up cups on trays for groups (add ice just before the activity):
- red-dot cup: Fill half full with rock salt, and add one spoon and popsicle stick.
- yellow-dot cup: Fill half full of ice.
- green **half**-dot cup: Fill half full of ice.

Introducing Ice Cream Ingredients
1. Tell students they will make secret formulas for ice cream next time. Discuss homemade ice cream. Ask them for attributes of ice cream, and list them.
2. Use data sheet on chalkboard to preview seven ingredients.
3. Say there are only two **flavors**—red, blue, and yellow are **coloring.**
4. Explain that everyone will get same amount of milk in cup and will choose quantity of other ingredients for their secret formula.

Modeling How to Add Ingredients
1. Use chalkboard data sheet to show maximum amounts.
2. Show your cup of milk. Model how to add and record ingredients.
3. Ask a volunteer to hold open a ziplock bag. Pour in mixture from cup and ask, "Is this ice cream?"
4. Ask how to make the ice cream cold. Clarify that ice isn't an ingredient of ice cream.

Introducing Rock Salt and Ice
1. Put your bag of ice cream ingredients aside, and use a tray of ice and rock salt to introduce the next activity.
2. Introduce rock salt. **Emphasize they are not to taste it.**
3. Say that they'll test what happens when they add rock salt to ice. Show yellow dot, and green half-dot cups of ice.
4. Say they'll add four level spoonfuls rock salt to yellow-dot cup, and leave the other cup just ice.
5. Say to put their fingers in cups of ice to feel which one is colder.
6. Quickly add ice to cups on trays and distribute. Have groups begin.
7. When all students have had enough time to feel the cups of ice for at least a minute or so, have them stop.
8. Regain their attention, and ask what they felt.

A Freezing Test
1. Each group will get two bags of water to put into their two cups of ice.
2. Show students how to bury water-filled corner of bag in ice cup.
3. Ask for predictions.
4. Distribute bags. After groups bury bags, they come to story-reading area.
5. Read story for at least 10 minutes. (Up to 20 minutes is fine.)

Checking the Results of the Freezing Test
1. Remind class that goal is to find out best way to make ice cream cold.
2. Have them check materials, then return to where you read the story.
3. Ask for observations. What should they use to freeze their bag of ice cream ingredients?

Clean Up
1. Have students dump ice into sink or dump bucket.
2. Rinse ice cups and air dry. Save cups of rock salt with spoons and popsicle sticks and your demonstration cups of ingredients.

Session 9: Secret Formulas for Ice Cream

Getting Ready
Before the Day of the Activity
___ 1. Decide where the students will shake ice cream. If indoors, have mop and bucket.
___ 2. Arrange for two or more adult volunteers.
___ 3. Ask one of the volunteers to make a few extra bags of ice cream.

On the Day of the Activity
Materials on Trays
___ 1. Prepare ingredient cups for each group:
  • blue-dot cup: about $^3/_4$ cup of sugar
  • green-dot cup: about $^1/_4$ cup vanilla extract (two ounces)
  • orange-dot cup: about $^1/_4$ cup strawberry extract (two ounces)
___ 2. Put two spoons and two popsicle sticks in each blue-dot cup. Put a dropper into each cup of extract.
___ 3. Add four stirrers to each tray.

Materials Not on Trays

___ 1. Post the color key from Session 8.

___ 2. Copy an Ice Cream data sheet for each student.

___ 3. Fill red-dot cups of rock salt from the previous session half full, and remove the spoons and stirrers. Have one cup per group, **not on the tray.**

___ 4. Fill one ziplock freezer bag about half full of ice for each group. Keep cold.

___ 5. With permanent marker, write students' initials on ziplock sandwich bags.

___ 6. Have personal cups clean and ready to pass out.

___ 7. Have milk ready in cooler.

___ 8. Prepare rinse bucket(s) and waste container.

___ 9. Have food coloring ready for adults to distribute.

___10. Have clean spoons for eating ice cream.

Reviewing Ingredients and Amounts

1. (*Optional*) Have students color code data sheets using color key as reference.

2. Tell students they'll get milk in personal cups up to bottom of initials.

3. Say to add a spoonful of sugar, stir, taste, circle data sheet, and repeat.

4. Review two flavors and maximum amounts. Urge students to smell flavors; once an ingredient is in, they can't take it out.

5. Review the color choices. [red, yellow, blue] Adult helpers will add these.

6. Review how to pour mixture into bag, and be careful bag is sealed well.

Explaining the Ice and Shaking Procedures

1. Each group will get an ice bag, pour in one red-dot cup of rock salt, then put in all four little bags and zip the ice bag very carefully.

2. Show how to put the ice bag into the T-shirt and shake it.

Let the Ice Cream Making Begin!

1. Student from each group gets tray of ingredients.

2. Helpers pass out personal cups and bags; adult pours milk into personal cups to bottom of initials.

3. Circulate, making sure they record ingredients added. Adult(s) add coloring and help seal bags.

4. Groups get ice bags, rock salt, and T-shirts, and begin shaking. Make sure everyone in group gets chance to participate.

5. As they finish, students dip small bags into rinse tub. Help students fold top of bag outward. **IMPORTANT: Make sure salt does not get into ice cream.**

6. Hand out spoons and have students eat. Ask how their special ice cream came out.

7. Collect bags, spoons, and clean up.

Name_____

Cola

My secret formula for cola is:

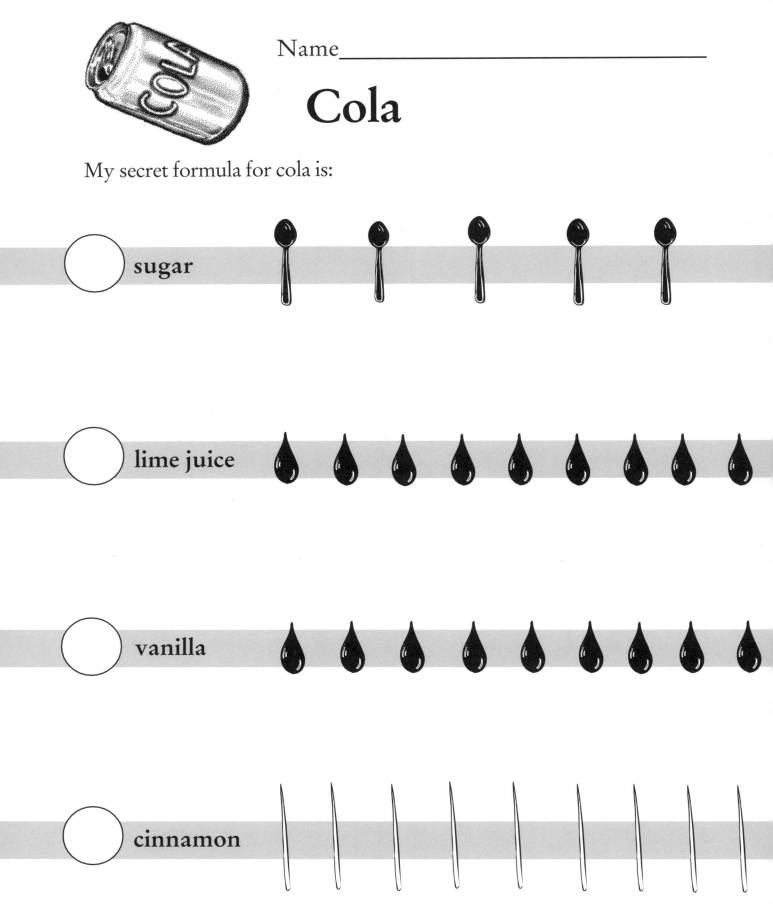

sugar

lime juice

vanilla

cinnamon

Name_____

Toothpaste

My secret formula for toothpaste is:

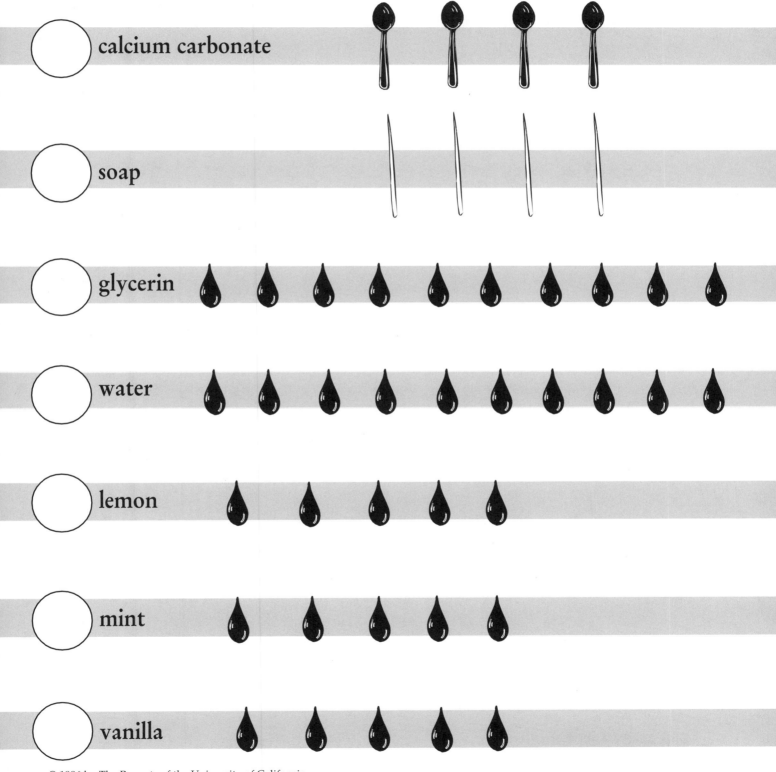

○ calcium carbonate

○ soap

○ glycerin

○ water

○ lemon

○ mint

○ vanilla

Name_____

Ice Cream

My secret formula for ice cream is:

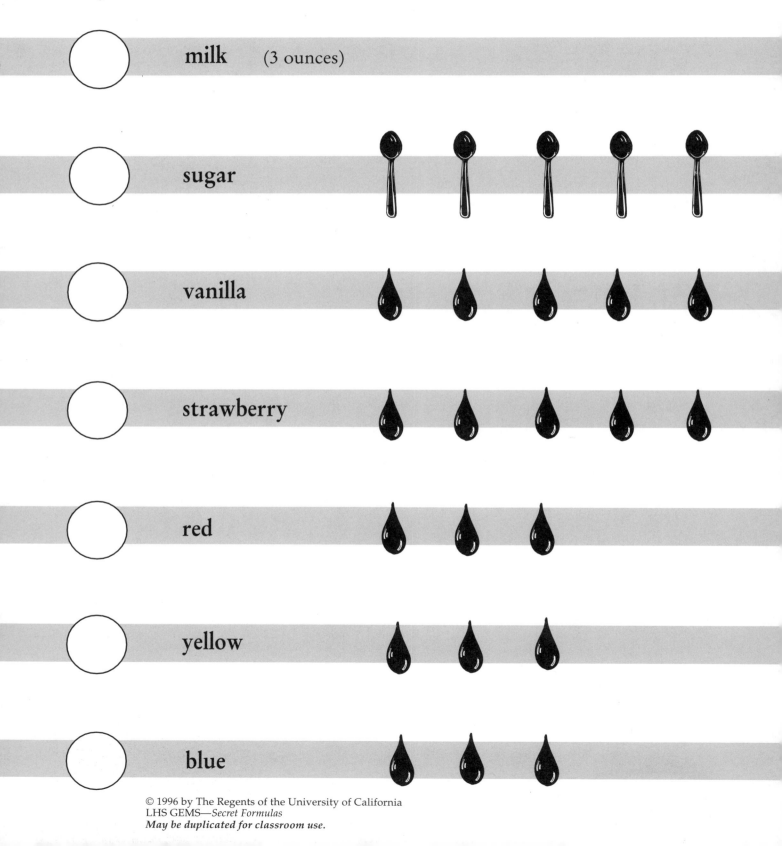

milk   (3 ounces)

sugar

vanilla

strawberry

red

yellow

blue